Dancing With God

First Year Thoughts
on the Loss of My Daughter

by Todd Stocker

A Special Thank You

To all of you who have walked the journey of loss and joy with my family and me, I say thanks! There are several people I'd like to thank by name ...

... My family (close and extended) who helped with the original blog editing and comments. I thank them most of all for their love,

... The Baltes and Stebbing families who encouraged me to begin writing my blog in the first place,

... Kristin Lock for her amazing computer compilation skills and Caitlin Cannon for her eye behind the camera,

... Mostly, the Lord's Spirit who gave me the words when I had none.

Our Story

My 18-year-old daughter, Makenzie, was a professional ballerina with the Bay Area Houston Ballet and Theatre. She and some of her friends decided to do a photo shoot by the water for fun. She donned her leotard, secured her long, false eyelashes and headed out the door to my parent's home on Taylor Lake in Seabrook, TX; the perfect setting to capture her graceful form. Everything went as planned.

The photographs were amazing. Poised on the dock, Makenzie and her dance partner jumped and leapt and "pirouetted" (whatever that is) as the camera froze them on film against the shimmering water and wispy pink sunset. Stunning.

At the end of the evening, they headed home. As was her habit, she called me to let me know she was on her way.

"Hi Dad. I had so much fun! I love you. I'm on my way home ..." She never made it.

An hour went by before I noticed that I hadn't yet heard the back door slam and her announcement, "I'M HOME!" I thought, maybe they had stopped to talk with my parents. Maybe they went out for a Jamba Juice (her favorite). Maybe she did come home after all and I didn't hear her glide upstairs to take a shower. So, I started texting her.

"I thought you were on your way home." No response. So I tried a few minutes later.

"You know you have to work tomorrow." Again, my cell phone was silent. Finally, we shot a final text to her:

"You better have a good reason for being late." She did.

At 8:08 that evening, only minutes after our last conversation, the car, in which she was a passenger, was broadsided and she was killed instantly. One moment, she was here; then next, she was gone. My beautiful daughter, who loved the Lord and was loved by so many, was taken to be with Jesus.

When my wife, Kellie, and I arrived at the receiving hospital, the E.R. staff immediately ushered us into the family waiting room and said they'd check on Makenzie' status. There we sat, or rather, paced. Just my wife and me, alone with our fears, questions and the Lord.

After several yearlong minutes, Kellie stepped out of our room and grabbed one of the police officers who was whispering to another in the hallway just outside the door.

"Can you please tell us what happened to our daughter! Is she all right? Can we see her?" The officer stepped in and said the words I thought I'd never have to hear: "You'd better sit down."

Honestly, I don't remember him telling us that Makenzie was killed in the accident. He didn't need to. I knew at that moment that our beautiful daughter, who was such a centerpiece of joy of faith in our family, was dead.

In the days that followed, our family ventured through emotions that I didn't know existed (or, at least, that I didn't think I'd ever experience). Pain, sorrow, and grief topped the list partnered with hope, love and confidence. Yes, you read that right; hurt and joy, loss and fullness. Feelings that don't normally grace my experiential halls together were walking hand in hand as I prepared to bury my daughter.

At Makenzie's celebration service, my son and youngest daughter spoke beautifully about their love for their older sister. Kellie and I closed out the service with some final words and I gave the blessing to the 1300 people in attendance. With tears streaming, everyone in the room knew that God was there and that He had gathered us to give us comfort and hope.

Soon after, we defied all the "professional" advice and moved our family back to Minnesota to heal. We stayed with friends for the first few months and then house sat through the long bitter winter. It was during this time that a dear friend of our suggested that an important part of healing may be to describe the day to day journey of grief.

What you'll find in the pages of this book are those remembrances; those deep down feelings, thoughts and prayers that kept me clinging to reality and surrender to my Savior.

Many of the posts lack the dialectic prowess of a scholar. Most are simply from my heart. They are unedited ramblings from a grief stricken dad who misses his daughter but knows she is ...

DANCING WITH GOD.

When All is Said and Done...

June 11

A week ago, I lost one of the most precious gifts God gave to me — my daughter, Makenzie. She was killed instantly in a car accident and my life will never be the same.

The outpouring of love on our family has been indescribable. Literally, hundreds of cards and texts have poured into the respective mailboxes and our home resembles a nursery. 1100 people took a last look at Makenzie at the visitation last Sunday and 1300 praised the Lord at her celebration service on Monday.

"God promises help in times of trouble."

Many people have asked me how I am managing to hold up; where my strength is coming from. When all is said and done, it only comes from what I know about God. God promises that whoever believes that Jesus is who he said he is and did what he said he did, doesn't die, but lives forever with him in heaven (John 3:16). God promises that he sends comfort and is an ever present help in times of trouble (Psalm 46). He has operated these promises in incredible ways this past week and we are OK.

When all is said and done, there is only one person on whom we cry; there is only one person to whom we turn and He is God.

Peace is Immediate… Healing is Slow

June 19

That title says it all. As soon as I found out that my 18 year old daughter was killed on June 3rd of this year, I knew she was with Jesus. That is where the PEACE came from. However, the pain and hurt was (and still is) incredible. We have been comforted by so many people from all over the world (literally) with condolences and prayers. One friend, who had suffered a similar loss, put our healing process this way. "Everyday we heal inch by inch." That is how we are healing today.

A Different Father's Day

June 21

This is a different Father's Day. In years past, Father's Day meant cut-out, hand-made cards, breakfast in bed and long morning hugs from my three children. This year is different. My kids have outgrown the handmade card artistry, I am awake long before they are wiping the sleep from their eyes, and the hugs will be a few less.

As I write this, I can't embrace what I'm feeling. (Frankly, I can barely put two sentences together). Like in a dance, the sense of loss and joy are twirling about the stage. I literally hurt, wanting to see my little Makenzie again and hear her shout "Happy Father's Day, Daddy!" like she had done every year since she could talk. I am so grateful that she gave me, and only me, those words.

I am so happy that God allows me the daily privilege of seeing Nathan grow into an incredible man. I am truly honored that God would give me an incredibly fun young girl in Maddie. Any dad would call himself blessed to have these two.

> "Makenzie is in the arms of her real Dad"

This is a different Father's Day. I won't get the kisses from Makenzie. I won't see her loving smile as she jumps on me to wake me from my sleep. And most of you have no idea how desperately I want one more squeeze from her. But I am reassured knowing that Makenzie is in the arms of her real daddy. (By the way — If God slept, she'd be planning to pounce on Him even as I write this).

Dad's — hug your kids extra tight today. I won't get to hug Makenzie again for a long time.

A New Day

June 23

We had dinner last night with a couple who lost their 16 year old son recently. The words they shared, their experience dealing with this kind of loss and their example of faithfulness and love were no less than inspiring. One of the most helpful discussions we had was the concept that every day, we heal a little bit more; ever day, we are strengthened by God.

This morning is a new day for me; a day when a little of the "pre-June 3" motivation is welling up; a day when the Bible verse comes to mind of God's new mercies...

> "Because of the Lord's great love we are not consumed,
> for his compassions never fail. They are new every
> morning; great is your faithfulness.
> I say to myself, "The Lord is my portion;
> therefore I will wait for him."
> Lamentations 3:22-24

In this new day, I will wait for God to renew me and I will remember that He is faithful. In this new day, I will be encouraged because His mercies and strength fulfill me and sustain me. In this new day, I will remind myself that His love and compassions are beyond understanding.

A Piece of Peace

June 25

After Makenzie's death this past month, many people have said to us, "I don't know how you do it. I couldn't be strong like you." In my guts, I wanted to say things like, "Sure you could ... You never know until you're in that situation ... Blah, blah, blah..." But now my response is, "You're right. You don't have the strength to get through having to bury your 18 year old child."

Now, I'm sure there is an innate reserve of human ability that God has hard-wired into each of us, but to dive deep into the dark waters of grief, that takes something that no human possesses; a peace that goes over and above any human understanding, resource or "positive thinking".

One thing is clear to Kellie and I right now: during the sad moments of the day when we look into the hole that has been punched through our family, God gives us what we need to get through it, not us. Sometimes, it's the knowledge that Makenzie is dancing for her King. Sometimes, its the warm embrace we find in each other. Ultimately, He gives us the ability to stare the pain of Makenzie's death right in the face and say, "God knows what He is doing!" We love Him more today and we did last month. We process our lives more today that we ever have in the past. And while none of this will bring Makenzie closer to us, it has definitely brought us closer to our Lord.

"The peace of God, which transcends all understanding, will guard your hearts and your minds in Christ Jesus."
Philippians 4:7

Talk Louder!

June 30

I was talking to a classroom of 3rd graders and wanted to get the point across that God loved them so so much. To do so, I lowered my voice —

almost to a whisper —

and said,

"You are loved".

I had them wrapped in wonder until a boy in the back yelled out, "Talk Louder!"

Since Makenzie's death, I've wanted to tell God, "Talk Louder!" I want Him to use His outside voice, inside me! More and more, I realize that God is talking but not necessarily louder. I can hear Him speaking in a friend who calls just to see how I'm doing. I

"You are loved"

can hear Him speaking in a song that gives me hope. I can hear Him speaking in the early morning as the sun is blossoming out from the horizon. I can hear Him speaking in the words of His love letter to me, "I will not leave you. I will not forsake you."

How Many Text Messages!?! (Part 1)

July 9

Yesterday, we received our phone bill on-line from the month of May. As is my habit, I looked at Makenzie's bill summary. 9713 text messages! That breaks down to 313 texts per day, 15 texts per hour. (Also remember that she was not texting – supposedly – during school hours of 7:30 – 2:30). Straight up... THAT'S A LOT OF TEXTS!

My first reaction was to fall down on my knees and thank God for the 'unlimited texting' feature on our family plan! But then I realized that my bill for June will show zero texts from her. I guess that's all part of the 'new normal' that we are getting use to. But we'd give anything to hear the "dut-dut-dut" of Makenzie's fingers dancing across the cell-phone keypad. We long to tell her to stop texting Katie at the same time she is talking to us! I smile as I write this and wonder, "Is there texting in heaven?"

How Many Text Messages!?! (Part 2)

July 13

In a few weeks, many families will be sending their first-born off to college. Many tears will be spilled. Many sighs will be heaved as they return home to a home-life that is different — changed from this point on. It's not good, it's not bad, it's just different.

> *"Is there texting in Heaven?"*

In a small way, I guess, these families have a taste of what our household is like now. There is a "new normal". There is one less person on the couch watching TV. There is one less person getting ready in the mornings or calling for "computer time." The biggest difference, as it comes to mind right now, is that the aforementioned families have two-way communication with their son or daughter whereas we have none. At any given moment, they can text for an update on dorm life, food, lack of money or just to get the all-important kid fix! We are satisfied in knowing the promises of God that "heaven is a wonderful place; filled with glory and Grace!" (I can hear you singing!)

I've appreciated that many of Makenzie's friends are still texting her phone. Most begin with, "I know you're not going to answer, but ..." and then they go on with sympathies, request for advice or just to know they are in communication with her. If you're one of those, DON'T STOP! We still love to hear her phone vibrate/ring. We still love to feel that she's going to answer it herself. And, truth be told, we love to be reminded that she is still alive, even if there's no texting in heaven.

The New Normal (Part 1)

July 14

I've spoken several times about this reality called the 'New Normal'. I don't exactly remember who said it but that phrase is not original. It was most definitely coined by someone who has already traveled this road on which we find ourselves.

Before June 3rd of this year, there was a life routine that defined our family life. There were certain activities, schedules and recreations that the five of us enjoyed. We knew, for example, that most nights around 8pm, Makenzie would pop in the door after several grueling but exhilarating hours of dance. We knew that in the early morning, Kellie and I could look up the stairs and see our three kids standing side-by-side in front of the mirror frantically combing, mousing and gelling their hair in an effort to be ready for school on time. We also could count on our three 'musketeers' sprawled out on Makenzie's bed, singing, laughing and processing all the struggles that Jr.

and Sr. High kids wrestle with until the early hours of the morning. But now, those normal activities of the past are different. We are thrust into the new normal.

Our new normal calls us to change everything. Our new normal celebrates those times in the past yet pulls us into the future. Our new normal laughs and cries with us but is not content to let us live in the 'before'. Our new normal has placed us in the 'after'. Our new normal, while new, eventually will be ... normal.

What we know for sure is that we are not wandering this forest of the new normal alone. The Lord was with us in our 'before', is with us in our 'now', and has already prepared for us our 'after'. In other words, God is always with us. We know that full well and love Him for it.

The New Normal (Part 2)

July 15

Part of the new normal has been to realize that it is natural for the old normal to show up. The other day, I went to set the table for dinner and pulled 5 plates out of the cabinet. I had to put one back.

Another part of the new normal is to notice when the old normal is absent. I grabbed the laundry out of the dryer and, after folding it, saw 4 piles instead of 5.

This new normal is becoming... well ... normal; minute by minute, day by day. We embrace it, reluctantly. We live it, reflexively. And each step we take together as a family, strengthens our bond and faith. God is so good. He gives... He takes away. And as the new normal seeps in and becomes our new lives, all that is left to say is, "Blessed be the name of the Lord." (Job 1:21).

The Heavenly Ballet

July 16

We have received so many wonderful sayings, songs and poetry that Makenzie's life inspired. Below is a poem that was written by Mary Neely called "The Heavenly Ballet."

She took the stage with grace and poise
Her audience awaited.
The music played, her body swayed
For this she was created.

> *As she moved across the stage*
> *Her soul and body, one.*
> *Her dancing took away our breath;*
> *The music had begun.*

The music stopped; she left the stage
Before the dance was finished.
Our hearts still beat, and we go on,
But life seems so diminished.

She takes the stage and once again
Her soul and body, one.
She dances with such glow and ease;
For her Father, Spirit, Son.

We'll miss her beauty and her joy
Forever and a day;
Until we dance beside her
In the Heavenly Ballet.

Sneak Attacks

July 19

On Friday, Kellie and I had coffee with Nancy and Katie – two of Makenzie's close friends. I asked how they were handling things after the accident that claimed Makenzie's earthly life. Katie said something to the effect of, "I'm OK except for those sneak attacks; those times when I come across a silly note that she wrote or a picture of her being a goof-ball. Then it hits me that she's not around anymore."

Every hour, I experience exactly what Katie said. I see reminders of Makenzie all over: pictures on the wall, car keys, a hair tie, and the countless bobby pins that seem to multiply like Tribbles (original Star Trek reference). How do I deal with it? Right now, I get weepy and tears cloud my eyes. But then I remind myself of all the promises of God. He promises that heaven is real. He promises that everything that happens is for the benefit of His kids. He promises that He will comfort us, even when those sneak attacks ... well ... are sneaky!

> *"God promises that He'll comfort us"*

We know Makenzie is not dead. We know she is alive with Jesus! We know that she is looking for the Marley floor on the streets of gold (if you're a ballerina, you know what I'm talking about). And, we know that we know that we know, that we'll be with her again in that Heavenly Ballet.

So let the sneak attacks come. I choose to face them head-on as a reminder, not of her death, but of her life!

What's in Your Closet?

July 21

Last week, we packed up Makenzie's bedroom. Not me. I couldn't. My gracious mother came over and helped Kellie. They didn't throw anything away (how could they) but they did box it all up for some future time of sorting.

But let me take you back to a day before the packing. Kellie, Nathan, Maddie, and I spent a solid two hours going through her "stuff." Let me tell you, it was a bitter sweet experience.

On the hangers inside her closet hung her uniforms and various "girl shoes" were scattered on the floor – just as she left them on June 3rd. We also came across a stack of her journals. Hidden away, we had no idea that she processed life on the pages. In them were her thoughts about life, people, relationships, school drama and the like. It was a fascinating look into her view of the world and the joy that she found in the everyday. Most of all, her journals showed that she knew two truths.

First, Makenzie knew <u>WHO</u> she was. She had a confidence in knowing that God made her to be, Makenzie. She knew that there were certain things she could and couldn't do but she emphasized the former. Faults? Yes. Shortcomings? Absolutely. And yet, she spoke of her audience of One. Whatever she did, she did it to please her Lord, Jesus.

Second, she also knew <u>WHOSE</u> she was. She knew that she was a "daughter of the King" (which is what her name, Makenzie, means). She knew that even though she couldn't be perfect, she could be loved. She knew even though others rolled their eyes at her heart for Jesus, He smiled.

This is just one of the many lessons that I'm learning from my own daughter. (Funny how the teacher becomes the student). What's in your closet?

The Word I Was Looking For

July 22

"The Lord is close to the _brokenhearted_ and saves those who are crushed in spirit." Psalm 34:18

That's the word I've been looking for; brokenhearted. I've been looking for it for a while. When asked how I'm doing, now I know; brokenhearted. It's the perfect word to label the feelings that sometimes wash over me. Without Makenzie, I feel brokenhearted. The sense of having someone you love and then, in a flash, they're gone.

There are reminders for me of my broken heart. When I see parents in Target, buying dorm room furniture for the college bound daughter ... brokenhearted. When I know that every Wednesday at 8:10pm, I'll remember how our lives were changed ... brokenhearted. When I call her cell phone and hear that cute voice, "Hi. This is Makenzie. I'm probably out dancing. You know what to do. Leave a message (beep)" ... brokenhearted.

But in the midst of it, the Lord is close. He is close to me and, as strange as it may seem, I have never felt so close to Him. The times when I feel crushed by the weight of the new normal in our lives, the Lord is close. And I'll always hold to the declaration, "He gives and He takes away. Blessed be the name of the Lord!"

My Bi-Polar Hope

July 27

It's not my medical condition. It's not my emotional state of being. It is how I, as a human Christian, have to deal with the loss of Makenzie. On the one hemisphere of my brain, I feel deep sorrow because I can't give her a hug; I can't hear her laugh; I can't watch her dance. On the other side of my noggin is the total joy that she isn't dead but alive; that I will get to see her again; I will give her a hug; I will be able to take a walk and chat with her. Sorrow and joy. Sadness and comfort. Grief and happiness. All dancing together on the stage of my emotions.

Those who have no hope, those who don't believe, deal with one emotion: despair. "My loved one was here but now gone and I am left trying to pick up the pieces." They have no option to look forward with hope. They have no sense that they will see mom/dad/grandma/daughter again. (Or if they do, it is underscored with the words "I think").

> *"My hope is real and my faith fills me up."*

My hope is real. My sadness is deep. My grief attacks me. My faith fills me up. Call me crazy if you want, but I'd rather live in the tension of loss and hope than in the futility of despair.

Instant

July 30

We received the autopsy on Makenzie the other day. (Wow, does that feel strange to say). What we had heard from the officers on the scene and other medical professionals was confirmed by the report; that Makenzie died instantly. As the euphemism goes, "She never knew what hit her."

When the impact happened, we believe that she was texting (big surprise) because on her phone was a last, unfinished text to her friend Wes that simply read "tomo..." She never saw the truck. She never heard the hit. The speed and power of the truck hitting the car at 63 mph snapped her into eternity.

The word that comes to mind is Instant. As quickly as you blink, as suddenly as you glance, Makenzie was looking at her cell and then looking at her Savior.

It all makes real the verse that says, "…we will all be changed— in a flash, in the twinkling of an eye…" (I Corinthians 15:51). Makenzie is alive with Jesus and we cant wait to see her again.

Going On Without Moving On

August 1

There are certain life events from which we move on: a bad math grade, an NBA championship upset, a betrayed friendship. To me, the phrase "moving on" means it's over and done with; in the past; don't look back. And in some sense, moving on is synonymous with "forget about it."

Makenzie's life-death-life is not something we just forget about. The impact she made on our family (and specifically, this daddy's heart) is not something we can leave in the past. I now know that we, who have experienced the death of our child, don't move on, we go on. We don't forget about her laugh, her smile, her joy. We don't pack away the light she carried into every room. We don't shelve the pain that every song, bobby-pin and picture brings. But we do go on with life because life demands it. I can't, nay, won't just move on. But I can go on, knowing that for 18 years, God gave me an incredible little girl who taught me to live a life of joy, even in the middle of sorrow.

I'm A Tree Hugger!

August 11

I've never wanted to hug a tree before; never really understood the purpose. (I don't even like granola or own a pair of hippie sandals). But this past Saturday, I was converted. As most of you know, we are staying at a beautiful cabin on a lake in MN; loons calling through the morning mist; bald Eagles riding the drafts high above the tree-lined shore; cool, sweatshirt mornings and warm, bathing-suit afternoons. A scene straight from the writings of Garrison Keillor and Lake Woebegone. Anyway, I digress.

Our friends, who own the cabin, picked out a spot on their land to plant a tree in Makenzie's memory. (She loved to spend time at that cabin). We found the perfect tree, dug the hole, prepared the soil and gathered around. All of us were overwhelmed with the sense of Makenzie's absence and God's presence. As the tears flowed freely, we heard the Lord speak to us from Psalm 30. We heard Makenzie's thoughts through one of her journal entries, sang through sobs and poured some of Makenzie's ashes around the base of the tree. This 20-minute celebration left us with an eternal sense that this was now holy ground. And I hugged that tree as if somehow I was hugging Makenzie herself.

So I have joined the ranks called "tree-huggers." And if I get a little bark on my clothes as I embrace Makenzie's tree, so be it. If I embarrass myself in front of the passing boaters and anglers, I'm fine with that. It's a small price to pay for the memory of an incredible young woman who has a dad on earth that longs for one more hug.

"We were overwhelmed with God's presence"

Uncleanliness Lead to Godliness

August 18

Pet Peeves. I have very few. But one that does get my proverbial goat deals with the inside windshield of my car. When humidity causes the inside of my car window to fog up, my natural reaction use to wipe it with my hand so I could see. Doing so left smudge marks when the condensation dried. I learned how to adjust the air conditioning vent to quickly dry up the water.

Somehow, I never covered that lesson when I taught Makenzie how to drive. Sure enough, streaks and marks appeared on the inside of my windshield within days of her officially taking the wheel. Even when I made her aware of my injurious pet peeve, she still managed to sneak a swipe now and then like defiant Nemo touching the bottom of the boat (or "butt" if you've seen the movie).

Fast forward (or rewind) to a few weeks ago; after the accident that claimed Makenzie's earthly life. It was a humid Houston morning. Like so many other mornings, I plopped down in my car, accidentally sloshing a few drops of steaming coffee onto the seat, and began thinking about the to-do list of my day. Inserting the key into the ignition, I started my car and looked up. There, on the humidified windshield were five thin finger marks, streaking from the center of the glass down to the dash-panel in a half-circled smudge. They were Makenzie's. Fingerprints that told her tale of disobedience. Smudges that proclaimed her independence. But I didn't care. I sat behind the wheel of my car, staring at the inside windshield, weeping uncontrollably.

They were (and still are) the last physical marks of my daughter and I vowed right there not to touch or clean them until driving safety required it. Pet peeve or not, Makenzie's smudges are symbols stating that sometimes, uncleanliness is next to godliness.

What A Weirdo (The First Day of School)

August 19

99.99% of school aged kids dislike school. Ok, maybe that's not a fair statistic but there are few people who really really enjoy going to school. Makenzie was one of those weirdoes. Makenzie LOVED school. Let me rewrite that ... Makenzie loved GOING to school. She did not always enjoy all the subjects (especially Math), but she loved the hustle and bustle of the day, hanging out with her friends and not-so friends, and all the mystery that each moment held. She loved knowing that she had the strength to live above the drama (even drama that she caused) and that at the end of the day, she could rest peacefully, knowing that God had walked right along side of her. In short, Makenzie loved life!

Truthfully, this was a difficult morning for Kellie and me. We watched the Facebook and texting entries of all the students preparing for that first day and wished that one from Makenzie would stumble across our screen. But even in the sadness, we know that those who knew her—and those who didn't—would be

> *"Makenzie knew that God walked right beside her"*

forever changed by that cute little weirdo, who loved God, loved life and even loved school.

Oh, if I could only be as weird.

Having Strength Before We Need It

August 24

Over these past few months of loss, love, transition and change, many people have said, "You both are so strong," and "We admire your faith," and "I could never be as strong as you."

I'll let you in on our secret.

A few weeks before the accident that claimed Makenzie's life, we attended a worship service at a church whose pastor and his wife were kidnapped in the Philippines while doing mission work. The series was called "Caught in the Crossfire." The message that morning dealt with preparedness. The pastor said that when you are in the midst of a tragedy, it's too late to prepare for it.

For years, unknown to us, God had been preparing us for the event that has redefined our lives. A long time ago, we began our days reading about this God who says He loves us. We began learning about this 'Divine Mentor' who opened our eyes to His power and grace. So at the time of the tragedy, we knew who was in charge and to whom we needed to turn. We knew that God is a god who wastes nothing and that this seemingly random accident has a purpose that is unfolding in the lives of all who knew Makenzie.

We don't need to ask the "why" questions because God told us that His grace is enough. We don't need to spiral down into the cold darkness of depression because God showed us the warm light of His love.

Our strength, in the middle of our loss, has been realized before June 3rd and carries us day-by-day; moment-by-moment.

> "I lift up my eyes to the hills — where does my help come from? My help comes from the LORD, the Maker of heaven and earth."
> Psalm 12

Family Reunion

September 10

All of us were stunned when we learned of the story of Jaycee Duggard. For those of you who didn't hear this story, Jaycee was abducted at the age of 11 and lived for 18 years in captivity by a man who, by all regards, is the personification of evil. Recently, investigators discovered the missing girl – now a woman – who had all but been forgotten and thought dead. It was phenomenal to watch the many news reports that told of her saga. I was especially drawn to the one of Jaycee's aunt who had just left the reunion meeting with Jaycee and her parents. The aunt, beaming with uncontainable excitement, spoke about the happy reunion. She said, "Jaycee and her family are in a safe place, reconnecting and getting to know each other again. Jayee's mom has a huge smile on her face and said, 'my oldest daughter is finally home.'"

If you've been reading my blog, you already know the connection that I am about to make. In a nutshell, Kellie and I can say the same thing as Jaycee's mom, "our oldest daughter is finally home!" Makenzie

> *"Makenzie is finally home with the Lord"*

is finally home with the Lord. No more sorrow; no more pain; no more wandering; no more shame. Makenzie is home. ("I Will Rise" by Chris Tomlin)

As I think about it. That was the last statement that she said to me before she died. "Hi Daddy. I love you. I'm on my way home." She had no idea how prophetic she was.

Today, I choose to take joy in the Family Reunion that we will experience in the future with Makenzie.

Surprised

September 11

Over the past few months, I've learned that people grieve the death of someone close the same but different. What I mean is there are natural human patterns or non-linear stages of grief that people experience: Denial, Anger, Bitterness, Depression, and Acceptance. I've cycled through most of these several times after Makenzie went home to heaven on June 3rd. While these are pretty standard for everyone, we land and take-off from these emotions at different schedules (Sorry...I'm on a plane writing this so I couldn't ignore the metaphor).

The reason this comes to mind is because I've been in Minnesota helping my youngest daughter, Maddie, start her first days of 7th grade. While she is doing wonderfully, both of us have experienced the same response from people when we meet and they find out about Makenzie. They are genuine in their grief for us but unsure how to react to when they see us smile. They are surprised to find that while we still hurt, while we still ache, while we still cry at the drop of a ... bobby pin, we still grin, laugh and even talk freely about Makenzie.

We are in the jet way of our new normal flight (sorry, again) and getting settled into the first leg of the journey ahead. We still miss Makenzie and always will. We still have our "Makenzie Moments" and still wonder what she's doing in heaven, but we are ok.

So when you see us, please know that we welcome your concerns and questions. Also know the joy that we have is given to us by the Master Himself.

Makenzie's Web

September 16

A friend of ours was pondering the amount of people that Makenzie's life affected. Realizing that the number was in the thousands, she said, "Makenzie had a web of influence that was beautiful and reached around the world. It's Makenzie's Web."

It reminded me of the delightful exchange between the spider, Charlotte, and the pig, Wilbur, in the classic story, "Charlottes Web."

Charlotte: Wilbur... we're born, we live, and when our time comes, we die. It's just a natural cycle of life.

Wilbur: No! Just climb down! I'll carry you the rest of the way! We'll go back to the barn and I'll take care of you!

Charlotte: No, Wilbur... I don't even have the strength to climb down...my webs were no miracle, Wilbur. I was only describing what I saw. The miracle is you.

Makenzie had a way of making everyone feel like they were a miracle (which, in fact, we are). From the popular kids at school, to the shy ones, by themselves, hiding in the corners. From the artsy to the jocks. From those possessing outstanding talent to those with none; it didn't matter. Makenzie's Web of love reached everyone who knew her and everyone just hearing about her story.

Makenzie's Web described what she saw in life as well. Joy instead of sadness; Love instead of hate; Freedom instead of guilt. And her web describes a life well lived, played out on the stage of this earth with an audience of One – her Savior, Jesus. She had a depth of love for Him that I, as a theologian, can't even grasp.

It makes me wonder how people would describe my web. Is it a web that experiences life as a great gift that God has given? Is it a web in which my family can grow and thrive? Is it a web defined by the love and grace of our Creator?

My Happy Birthday

September 17

Birthdays come and birthdays go. Some I celebrate; others are swallowed up by the busyness of life. Today is one of the latter for me and that's fine. It is one of the many "first's without ..." that I'll experience over the next years as I continue my journey into the new normal.

As I was flipping through Makenzie's journals, one entry caught my eye and called out to me as I celebrate my birthday today. Written a few years back, her words are a sweet sound to this daddy's heart.

Dear Diary,

Tomorrow is my dad's 41st birthday. Can you believe it!? It seems like yesterday I was 7 years old, sitting on his lap, playing with his hands and watching Barney! I really want to show him how much I love him! He's always been here for me. He has always laughed when I say I wanna be just like him but it's true; I do. He really understands me and is a perfect example of God. I love him so much and I hope he knows that. I'm not just a normal teenage girl who would normally forget all about her dad. But my dad's awesome cause he reminds me what I want to be like everyday!

I love you too, Makenzie. I love you too.

Tears For No Reason

September 21

In the past, my tears partnered with a specific event; I hit my finger with a hammer – tears; I watched the end of "It's a Wonderful Life" – tears; I witnessed the Minnesota Gophers throw away an opportunity to knock off Cal – tears. Yesterday was different. My tears trailed down my 40+ year old wrinkles and I didn't know why.

Let me take you to Sunday afternoon.

"I celebrate God's work in our family"

My youngest, Maddie was standing at the light oak rail of my former church, receiving the Lord's Supper for the first time. Surrounded by our family and friends, the setting was Hallmark-ish. As the Pastor read scripture, talked about the significance of the meal and prayed for God's Spirit to permeate Maddie's life, they came once again – tears. Maybe it was the realization that I was standing on holy ground; maybe it was my fatherly pride welling up as I saw my lovely Maddie; maybe it was the incredible sense of acceptance that I felt from our friends. Or maybe it was the unspoken reality that one, in our family, was not there to wrap her arms around Maddie and whisper, "I'm so glad I'm your sister." Maddie would've loved to hear it. I would've loved to seen it. But that hug and those words will just have to wait.

As I sit quietly and think on yesterday, the tears come once again. And, as before, I'm still not quite sure why. I guess I don't need to know. I only need to celebrate God's work in Maddie and our family and trust that today, it's ok to have tears.

Not Shaken

September 23

Already, my thoughts are turbulent. As the sun bubbled up over the horizon and spilled out onto this morning's canvas, feelings of uncertainty, sadness and loss battled for control of my emotions. Thankfully, God brought to mind the lyrics to a song we sang at church this past Sunday. The song was "You're Not Shaken" by Phil Stacey.

The moving melody backdrops words that speak of pain and suffering from which the singer knows not where. The message is clear that when everything seems to be crashing down and there are no answers to the questions, that God is still there; He never leaves; He's at my side. And when my world is a quake, my God is not shaken.

What is so real to me after Makenzie's death is that when my life is chaotic, God brings sanity. When I feel unsteady, God is not shaken. And I continue to ask, "What do people do that don't have the Lord?"

Feeling Guilty for Not Feeling Guilty

September 23

I think I have issues. You see, I've always been a light-hearted person. More or less, I've had a positive view of life; a silver-lining vs. cloud-encompassing mentality. After Makenzie went home to be with Jesus a few months ago, I wasn't sure if there would be any residue of my joy intact. These days, I've found the Lord has preserved my heart and I actually hear myself laughing again. (Psalm 51:12).

But is it ok to be able to laugh without guilt while still in the wake of a parent's worst nightmare? Today, I didn't care what the textbooks said; I laughed. How couldn't I? Celebrating Maddie's 13th birthday brought out the giggles in me again. I found ironic humor in eating a perfect chocolate mousse cake as the Olive Garden staff butchered a rendition of Happy Birthday. That made me laugh. I realized the beautiful picture of the four of us talking about the new-revised-standard-version of our family and eating

only the buttery part of the bread sticks. I laughed again...
out loud (LOL)! And at that moment, it felt good.

> "Sometimes I feel guilty for not feeling guilty"

The truth is, sometimes I feel guilty for not feeling guilty. But that initial feeling is relieved in knowing that Makenzie would have wanted us to laugh; and laugh hard. She would have wanted us to celebrate her sister's special day because she loved her. And it is that thought that makes me want to laugh again.

That Family

September 28

Last weekend, Kellie and I were surrogate parents at Iowa State's parent weekend for Alex, the young man Makenzie took to prom in March. (His mom and dad were out of town). We went to the football game, toured the sprawling campus, and met several of Alex's friends. It was loads of fun.

During our time, we decided to check out the campus bookstore. The place was packed with parent-toting students, shuffling through the well-supplied shelves and strategically placed display tables. Other college-aged workers were scampering through the crowd in a futile effort to keep items on the shelves, stopping only to answer the occasional "dumb" question from a mom or dad.

As I sifted through the racks of t-shirts, hoodies and various I-State paraphernalia, I noticed one family that reminded me of what ours use to look like. There was mom, dad, youngest daughter, middle son and oldest daughter; a freshman, I assumed, as she was still enthralled with the newness of everything around her. They were standing at a clothing stack. The mom was holding up a t-shirt against the back of the son for an informal fitting. The dad was thumbing through the various logo imprinted coffee mugs and the three kids were chatting phrases to each other, "This looks cool." "How do I look in this?"

Then a "Makenzie Moment" hit me. Makenzie loved to shop (although she rarely took the opportunity). Just like the freshman that stood before me in the campus bookstore, she loved to shop with her younger brother and sister. I could picture my three, together, standing in the aisle of Marshals debating whether the random faded-ness on a pair of faded jeans was too ... faded. Nathan would say the shirt that Makenzie had picked out was gauche while Maddie would grab whatever was within finger-reach and ask, "What about this one, Makenzie?"

Standing there, in the I-State campus bookstore, I allowed the other family's interaction to transport me back to the aisles of Marshalls. I fought down the lump that was welling up in my throat as I realized I would never experience that scene again with my own kids — not with all three of them anyway. And as I watched these other kids bickering over clothing style and heard the Dad say, "Ok, that's enough," I so desperately wanted to tell them to enjoy this moment. I wanted to push through my shyness to impress upon them that every moment together is golden and that it is enough just to be together. I regret my hesitation.

So, to that family, if you're reading this, (which, I suppose, you very well could be) thank you for bringing me back to a memory that etched a smile on my face. Thank you for reminding me that even though our family is not the same, we are ok. And remember, I-State family, hug your kids because you never know when it will be the last one you give.

In the Middle of the Struggle

September 30

For the past few months, I've taken you on a journey of grief, struggle, joy, and hope. I've shared my desperate ache at the loss of my daughter, Makenzie and I've tried to explain what pain and gain feel like as they stroll, arm in arm, through my emotional hallway. Sometimes, I've been successful; Other times, my words are thin.

But a friend of mine wrote the following that expresses what many of us, who knew Makenzie, now feel:

"A couple of years ago, I took a newly-widowed friend of mine from to a speech from a grief expert. He started off his talk with a whopper that made everyone in the room (all grieving a loss) just lose it. **He said he's accepted the loss of his loved one the person, but struggled to accept the loss of the dreams he had with/for that loved one....that's where all of his pain was."**

This speaker was right on. I can say that "...I've accepted the loss of Makenzie, but I struggle to accept the loss of the dreams I had with/for her." I struggle knowing that the homecoming dance at her high school in Houston is coming up and I won't see her try on every dress that she could borrow from friends. I struggle to see that family together at Iowa State University, knowing that I won't experience Makenzie's freshman year in college. I even struggle having fun as a family because I so desperately want to tell Makenzie how goofy her brother and sister were being.

I guess Job said it best ...

"Is not all human life a struggle? Our lives are like that of a hired hand, like a worker who longs for the shade, like a servant waiting to be paid.
I, too, have been assigned months of futility,
long and weary nights of misery."
Job 7:1-3 (New Living Translation)

But today, I am glad that God is a God in the midst of the struggle. He is not the spectator in the stands; He is the warrior on the field. And in the midst of my struggles, He tells me that everything is going to be ok (John 14).

Bearing it All... Almost (Part 1)

October 5

I've received so many wonderful emails in response to Makenzie's Living Magazine article.

One person wrote ...

"Today I was so angry at my daughter for not cleaning her room and was irritated during most of the day. As I found and read your article about your storm in the CyFair Living Magazine, tears just flowed and flowed out of my eyes and I ached in my heart for you. I am going upstairs to kiss and hug my daughter. I will tell her about Makenzie. Thank you so much and may God bless and strengthen you!"

And another said,

"Todd, I read about your story in the Keller/Metroport Living Home and Family Style Life and was moved. Thank you for sharing this and for glorifying the Lord during this season. He is worthy of all of our praise, isn't He!"

> "*God is worthy of all of our praise, isn't He*"

It isn't easy sharing this unintended journey that our family travels. Much of it is good. Some of it is incredibly painful. But over these months, it has been helpful for me to open up a bit and let you peek into the windows of our grief and joy.

Believe me, there is many windows into which I don't allow you to look. Truthfully, there are many closed emotional shutters that I, too, walk by. Eventually, I'll be strong enough to at least lift the shade, but not now. It's only been 4 months 4 days 12 hours and 12 min since my life was changed forever and I'm not in a rush to be hurt like that again.

Bearing it All... Almost (Part 2)

October 6

When Makenzie died this past June, I never realized how deeply that wound cut. In my mind, I thought, "Ok, after a few weeks, things should be back to 'normal.'" Foolish thought; especially in response to the loss of someone who brought so much joy to my life and the rest of the entire planet.

It would've been easy to lock myself away and not be open about what God has allowed to happen. (Truthfully, there are too many days, now, that I feel like doing that). But it has been helpful for me to write and talk about Makenzie; to let you see into my 'home.'

A friend of mine wrote an email that captures this idea from an outside perspective:

"Voyeur, peeping tom, trespasser ... that's how I feel sometimes when I read your blog. Part of me doesn't want to read it. Another part of me wants to. Depending

on the day, one of them wins. And there are those moments where I feel like I am invading your privacy, looking into a window of a house from the street, hiding in the dark because I don't leave a comment...

I feel like I have stepped into the holy of holies of someone's grief, a place typically off limits. . But then I am reminded you have invited me in, opened the door, even ripped the curtain from to top to bottom just to let us in. I feel like I shouldn't be here but you have said come on in. I am reminded of Christ death, the torn curtain, the holy of holies and having full access to God. It feels like I should be there but I have been invited in by His grace and through His pain.

Most people don't do what you are doing. Most people rarely share. Seldom, even as a pastor, are you invited in. But then you are not most people and I thank God for that. Thank you for showing us grace and inviting us in ... even into the pain. You are profoundly changing people's experience with grief, grace and even God!"
- Pastor Brad Heintz, Living Word Church - Houston, TX.

My Idle Mind is Makenzie's Playground

October 8

I know. The title does not reflect how my grandmother's chiding went. For me, the statement seems true today. As I sit here sipping Java, Makenzie's image tip-toes into my idle mind. Look. There are her beautiful green eyes, peeking out from the curtains of the empty stage of my thoughts. I see her mischievous smile warning me that she's about to pounce.

"Ta Da!" Makenzie loved to make an entrance.

My thoughts flip through the past pages of my memory. I see Makenzie, holding up her 4 year old arms above her leotard-donned frame. She is skipping from one circle to another on the Marley floor of her first dance class. I see her pushing Nathan, then Maddie in the now, government-recalled stroller. She is announcing to the passersby, "This is my Brother/Sister!" as if they were royalty.

"Bye Daddy; I love you"

Now I see her swimming with her 8th grade class in our backyard, Arizona pool and I hear her deep, snorty laugh when her "friend-who-is-a-boy" tells her a joke. I see her dancing on the beach with her cousins and I see her snuggling her way in-between Kellie and me, begging, "Keep me warm, Mommy." And, finally, I see her walking out the door that last time, planting a smooch on my cheek saying, "Bye Daddy; I love you."

Those who've lost people they love have these same times of idleness. We have those moments when we find ourselves wandering the paths of the past, hoping we won't meet our daughter/brother/parent's memory - it's disabling — but there they are. Those mental pictures of the one we love so deeply. Those desires that yearn, "if only they were here."

As I'm told, those thoughts don't, and won't go away. Sometimes, they are a menacing gift — a beautiful curse. If you're on my same journey, you've allowed your mind to empty the stage and wait for your performer. You aren't sure if you'll be able to handle what your memory shows you or if this will just be another happy thought. But trust me, we are not watching this play alone. Look to your left. Do you see Him? He is sitting next to you, compassionately looking at you, and He is holding out the Kleenex box. As the curtain closes on my idle stage, my Lord says, "I'll be right here for the next performance." (Psalm 139:7-9)

Cast All of Your Cares... Into a Basket?

October 16

This morning, Kellie gifted me with an hour-long massage at the spa residing in our hotel. Swanky and relaxing, the spa had all the accoutrement one expects when spending money just to have a back-rub. Anyway, as I walked into the dimly lit room, Natasha (yes, that's her real name) invited me to disrobe, climb under the covers that were draped neatly over the massage table and relax after she had given me a few private moments. Now, I have had a few of these things before so I sort of knew the drill. But this time, her exit was different than what I expected. As she was leaving, she pointed to a little, wicker basket that hung by the door. Woven into and hanging down from the rim of the basket were tattered, stringy braids; each ending with a sachet filled with pebbles, dried flowers and pixy dust. (Ok, probably not pixy dust but who knows; this is the epicenter of "spirituality," so they say).

As Natasha pointed to the oddly hanging decoration, she said, "This is a burden basket. When you're ready, place all your burdens, worries and cares in there and we'll hang it outside the door. That way you can be totally relaxed."

Have you ever tried to hold back a sneeze and afterward, you thought you ruptured something,

"Cast all your anxiety on Him"

somewhere that might be important someday? For me it wasn't a sneeze, but a laugh. Is she serious? I thought. First of all, the burdens, worries and cares of a 2 year old wouldn't fit in that thing. Secondly, just the thought of trying to put our families burdens of these last months into a three-dollar, Pier One overstock item, just made me laugh. What; then outside the door, the basket magically transforms my cares and hurts into happy thoughts?! I don't think so.

I'd rather give them to someone who knows what it means to suffer. I'd rather place them in the nail-pounded hands of the one who gave everything for me. I'd rather let Him give me the Peace that goes beyond my imagination than let a mass-manufactured pixie dust holder pretend to give me hope.

I walked out of the room — post-massage, of course — relaxed and refreshed, thanking the Lord for being ready to receive my stress. I guess I didn't need a massage for that; but it sure was nice.

"Cast all your anxiety on him because he cares for you."
1 Peter 5:7

A Time to Mourn

October 19

Makenzie had a web; one that reached so many people in so many different parts of the county. Because ministry had moved our family so many times, Makenzie interacted with hundreds of different people. When she suddenly went home to heaven on June 3rd of this year, those hundreds – now thousands – needed to mourn; however that looked, whatever shaped that took, we all need to mourn the death of those we love.

Yesterday, Kellie and I were given the privilege, once again, of sharing Makenzie's story with the people of Summit Community Church in Buckeye, Arizona. It was a time to weep and a time to laugh; A time to mourn and a time to dance. (I love that the NASB version of the Bible uses the word "dance"). As we spoke, I knew that somehow this was closure for our Arizona church family. This was their time to see, hear and hug on us as a way to say goodbye to one of their daughters of the church.

Each of us has to have a time to mourn. Whatever loss is woven into the fabric of our futures, each of us has to have a time to weep. In my minds eye, I see one of Makenzie's fellow classmates from 8th grade, finally letting out all of his sorrow on Kellie's shoulder as she wrapped him in her arms. I can also see one of my former ministry team leader's tear-reddened eyes look deep into mine as she struggles to say how sorry and saddened she was. It is all good. It is all healthy. It is all part of the human experience called "loss."

All of us need to have a time to mourn.

"There is a time for everything,
and a season for every activity under heaven:
a time to weep and a time to laugh,
a time to mourn and a time to dance,"
Ecclesiastes 3

Time Marches On

October 22

Yesterday, it happened again. And I noticed the same thing today. In the morning, the sun strolled up and out from sleeping behind the horizon. At mid-day, the clouds sauntered across the sky. Into the evening, the wind hushed it's howling and Day graciously released her dominance to Night. Minute by minute, hour by hour, time marched on.

Ever since the accident that claimed Makenzie's life on June 3rd, I've clung to the romantic hope that time would not move; that the gears in my clocks would not push the hands around it's face. Silly notion – I know. But every click that marks the seconds is one more click away from my daughter being physically with me. Like the rabbit in "Alice In Wonderland," Mr. Time has taken me farther and farther from celebrating her 18th birthday this past May. He has pulled me beyond watching my beautiful girl float around at prom like a Princess. He has faded the aroma of her hair, the sound of her voice and the feel of her hugs. Time is a relentless eraser.

> "*Time is a relentless eraser*"

So, it could be that time is now my enemy; carrying me farther from my past with Makenzie and presenting me to my future without her. However, because of the promise that God made me, Makenzie is not not in my tomorrows. Because she knows Jesus, believes in who He is and makes Him her King, Makenzie is living in His presence in the heaven that will one day be my home. Imagine; experiencing life with no sadness – no feeling of loss. Imagine; relationships that are pure and without envy or pain. The heaven that only Jesus can give is the totality of perfection, and … There will be no clocks.

Good Try

October 26

They say that the fifth month following the death of a child is the one of the hardest. Generally, in month one, the novelty of the loss wears out. In month two, we go back to our jobs, routines, and daily life. Month three and four show us what has changed and a new normal is born. In month five, we are faced with the reality that there is a huge hole in our lives; that things aren't the same. And we look back over our shoulder in hopes that the preceding months were simply someone's bad joke.

October has been month five since Makenzie "cut in line." While my experience

"Makenzie cut in line"

in the hinterland of Minnesota has been good, it has also been pressing. Makenzie loved it up here. She loved the change of seasons. She loved the "Minnesota Niceness." She loved the snow. (Where did she get that gene from?!)

So moving north has kept me from reopening the scab of loss that I felt in Houston. But it has also reminded me – especially in month five – that life, right now, is very, very different. Month five has been waiting his turn to dig up my grief. He has tried to get in my face, saying, "God must not care," and "Looks like you're on your own." That's crap.

Month five is leaving at the end of this week. He tried to bury our family in despair this month but he did not succeed. He was outsmarted by a different friend of our family that God's Holy Spirit has allowed to come back home. Someone that, for years, has helped heal our wounds, relational hiccups and painful routines. A friend that helps us realize that joy is still alive and that everything is going to be ok.

I'm glad he's back ... and I'll introduce you to Him later this week.

I'm Back!

October 28

"He will yet fill your mouth with laughter and your lips with shouts of joy." Job 8:20-22

I don't know how it started or who let him in, but somehow, without warning, there he was. Laughter. Our friend from former days. Laughter. The one in our family who sat quietly during the past months as tears and weeping took their turn, helping us heal; helping us cope with Makenzie's death. But this past weekend, Laughter jumped off the couch and rejoined our family.

It was just the four of us, huddling together at a cabin in northern Minnesota. Kellie and Maddie were playing Dutch Blitz – a card game only crazy people like – and Nathan and I were munching on chips. Before long, I noticed my gut hurting and my cheeks stained with tears. No, not the swine flu, but the result of mouth-wide-open, head-tilted, eyes-shut, full-out Laughter. This wasn't

> *"He will yet fill your mouth with laughter"*

Laughter's little cousin, Giggles. This was really him! Back again. And maybe it was something Nathan said. Maybe it was something Kellie or Maddie did. All I know is that whatever 'it' was, Laughter took the opportunity to bring his joy back into our family.

The pain is still around. The moments of grief sometimes still consume us. But God has given back our longtime friend and it feels good.

Tributes

Makenzie danced all over the United States. Missouri, Minnesota, Arizona, Louisiana, Texas, New York; many were affected by this little ballerina named Makenzie. As a result of her influence and after she was killed, tributes of all sorts were created by those who love her. Youtube hosts many of these done by her fellow classmates and me as well. Dance studios have choreographed pieces in her memory as a tribute to a life well lived and cut short. Last Saturday, the Minnesota Classical Ballet Academy – where Makenzie danced in grade school – dedicated a dance choreographed to Mozart's Symphony No. 40 in honor of Makenzie.

Within the context of the performance, a little girl occasionally walked on stage, mingled through the dancers and stood to the side, watching the others turn and move to the music. At one point, the little girl wearing lavender (Makenzie's favorite color) knelt down and recited the words to our families evening prayer.

"Now I lay me down to sleep; I pray the Lord my soul to keep. If I should die before I wake; I know the Lord my soul will take."

We couldn't hold back the tears and they washed down our faces as we were again reminded of Makenzie's purity, faith and joy. Surrounded by our friends, we watched the little 'Makenzie' stand up and be carried off by a man in white (God) as the dancers continued to perform with passion and grace.

At the end of the dance, as the last chord faded into the air, all of the performers slowly made their exit, save one. A lavender sashed ballerina, on pointe and back facing the audience, gracefully tiptoed off-stage, leaving an empty space the size of the one in our family. Wonderful. Stunning. Symbolic. Painful. But Beautiful as well. A tribute to my little ballerina who is dancing arm in arm with Jesus.

UP

November 12

I don't know if you've seen the movie UP. If you have offspring still hovering around your kneecaps, my guess is, you have. A wonderful story put to film about an older man who vows to finish a dream he and his wife held before she died; to live in their house next to Paradise Falls.

Accompanied by an unwanted boy scout (Russell), the old man and little boy fight evil talking dogs, treacherous paths and a long lost aviator turned lunatic.

Throughout the 90 minute film, we laughed and cried and cried some more. For whatever reason, the movie

"All God asks us to do is to look UP"

hit us hard. Maybe it was the realization that this was the last movie that Makenzie and Maddie saw together. Maybe it was the scenes of the old man sitting alone in his chair next to his wife's. Maybe it was the clear message of letting go of the past and going on into the future. It was probably a combination of it all. But we wept. All four of us. Wept. We wanted Makenzie there to share in our family time. We wanted to see her crinkled nose and hear her snorty laugh. We all wanted Makenzie.

But just like in the movie, we have to celebrate our past and live in the present. God has given us a chance to begin again and move into the future, bringing Makenzie's memory with us. He is the one leading us where He desires us to go. He is the one who sees our full journey. And all He asks us to do is to continue to look ... UP (Hebrews 12).

Ecuador- We Made It!

(In the spring, Makenzie collected 2,000 pairs of shoes from her classmates to bring down to the poor in Quito, Ecuador. After the accident, our family decided to finish what Makenzie started. As a result, Kellie, Nathan, Maddie and I flew to Ecuador during the Thanksgiving break to work with our friends, Brad and Sandi Miller and deliver the shoes. Calling our venture "Soles for Souls," we chronicled our endeavor)

November 21

Just a quick update to let everyone know that we made it safe and sound. God is already at work. He smoothed out the details of the flight, getting the shoes (and turkey) through Ecuadorian customs and connecting with Brad and Sandi Miller. Today is a day of acclimating to climate and culture.

I'll be doing evening or early morning updates.
Thanks for the prayers.

Ecuador Day 1: Kenzie Would Have Loved This!

November 21

"Kenzie would have loved this!" How many times has that phrase bounced around in my thoughts over the past few months as our family discovers it's new normal without her. On this occasion, that phrase is bouncing off the well worn plaster walls of the small streets of Quito, Ecuador.

At around 9,000 feet, the first day in Quito has been spent acclimating to the said altitude and culture. Past experience warms me not to do anything strenuous right away when entering into a different part of the world. Not heeding that wisdom, we climbed eight stories up to the top of the Basilica and bobbled across the dusty planks of her attic. Maybe it was the view; maybe it was the lack of oxygen, but my knees felt jiggly as I stopped and looked out across this city that is only five miles wide but twenty-five miles long. Breathtaking! Below us, some sixty feet, the muffled sound of Gregorian chant seeped through the cracks of the historic trusses.

"Kenzie would have loved this!"

The Millers brought us into the old city of Quito. 'Old' here does not mean built in the 1950's. We're talking buildings built in the 1650's and original food recipes that I can't even pronounce. Fresh fruit juices, empanadas and street baked peanuts and potato chips filled our tummies us as we strolled through the cobblestone street of the historic La Ronda.

"Kenzie would have loved this!"

As the hot morning sun gave way to the cold afternoon wind, we headed back to the Miller's and processed the day. Great friends, food, culture, history, and great anticipation as we think about what the Lord has in store for us tomorrow. And yes, "Kenzie would have loved this!"

Ecuador Day 2: Sameness

November 23

I was surprised to find the word used for the title of this blog was actually ... well ... a word! Loosely, the word sameness means having qualities that are similar or the same in comparison to others. Such was my experience — or maybe awareness — of day two in Quito.

"God is unpredictable"

Much of the time, God is unpredictable. He does stuff, creates stuff, and has me experience stuff that I never expected. But when we stepped into worship at Monte Zion Iglesias Christiana (church) we found the same Lord being worshipped and praised. Yes, the setting was different and yes, it was all in spanish, but the sameness of the Holy Spirit guiding our hearts in praise was nothing short of breathtaking. (Frankly, I understood more of the Spanish message that I did many of the English ones I've heard). People loved on each other. People loved on us. We greeted each other with a 'holy kiss.' And it was beautiful.

After lunch — I mean 'feast' — we went to the market. Brad and Sandi noticed the increased *Polici* presence throughout the one-and-a-half person wide aisles of shops. I felt safe. Nathan bought hats. Maddie negotiated with the vendors and Kellie spent all of my money (did I just say that out loud?). But the people were people. Not some strange creations from a distant planet. They were God-created, God-inspired, God-loved people. The sameness of daily frustrations (albeit deepened by their desperate plight) etched lines of concern around the tight skin on their faces. The sameness of trying to make a living and doing the best they can for their families inspired them to sell the handmade cloths, sweaters and trinkets in their family shops.

Darting in and out of the familiar tourist crowds, shoeless four and five year-old children stopped only to look up to get a bearing of where they were. Some carried little boxes of gum to sell to those of us who would look down and take notice.

For me, I connected with a shop owner who was the sole holder of coffee mugs in the 30 or so rows of proprietorship. He laughed at my very weak effort at speaking Spanish and I laughed because I felt completely at his mercy. Purchasing the home-made mug, we exchanged a hand shake, a "dios te bendega" (God bless you), and I knew that God loved both of us the same.

The poverty is great here. The people are as well. And I feel a little humbled that I am now part of their world and not the other way around.

Ecuador- Day 3: Hands On

November 24

It is early as I write this and words are not quick to dribble off my fingers. So permit me to describe my Day 3, Quito experience using the words of Jeremy Bautista ...

"Dump ministry. I didn't know what that really meant, even though its been talked about often. First of all, its important to understand what happens at the Dump. When someone throws out their trash, they put it outside their house. Someone is sure to go through it looking for anything valuable from things to resell, recycle, or eat. After that, the trash collectors (similar to those I know of in the States) take the trash, sort out what they want for themselves (in bins above the main trash hold), and dumps the rest of the trash out in the garbage truck. The garbage truck then delivers the leftover trash to the Quito City Dump (now called a Transfer Center). Each truck dumps its trash where it is then sorted out again. The people who sort through this trash call themselves miners. They too collect anything that they want for themselves including food and recyclables to be sold (i.e. plastic

bottles, paper, metal, etc.). They get paid pennies to the pound and usually only eat what they find."

Ok, me again. (Thanks Jeremy). One of the ministries to the workers that Jeremy describes above is a daycare center for their children. Previously, the children were either strapped to their backs for 12 hours at a time or dashing around the garbage piles, scavenging for food, toys or anything that looked interesting. Developed by Extreme Response, this place gives the kids 3 meals a day, relational contact with others, and basically helps raise them in an environment that is safe. Many of them go home to dirt floors and tin walls.

We spent our day, playing with them, changing diapers, singing, playing guitar, and just having fun. On the advice of Sandi Miller, we prayed for them even though they had no idea what we said. Doesn't matter. The Holy Spirit isn't bound by language!

At the end of the day, the little ones filed two-by-two into the on-site Pastor's office where our family gave them a new pair of shoes. Having developed a relationship with them during the hours before, it took the last ounce of strength in me to hold back tears as little Miguel, Daniel, Esperanza and Michelle came into the room. Their eyes popped open when they saw the shoes. And when we pulled off their tattered foot coverings and gave them new ones, I knew that what we take for granted in the states, they hold as treasures in Ecuador.

This is why we are here. No, not just to give away shoes, but to connect and pray and follow Jesus

"We are simply to pray and follow Jesus"

where He leads us. I never would have thought that what our beautiful Makenzie started this past spring, would be fulfilled in such a powerfully simple way. Who knows what Day 4 holds for us. We have a plan but in Ecuador (and in God's economy), we hold it loosely.

Ecuador- Day 4: The Boys of Casa G.

November 25

Brad and Sandi Miller are serving with Youth World, an arm of International Teams. Brad oversees the organization that has five branch ministries. Each of these have different yet powerful emphasis on reaching people for Christ. Day 4, we went to a place that focuses on getting boys off of the streets, leading them to Christ and helping develop in them a lifestyle of love, respect, integrity and servant leadership. During our orientation, the director explained that the home (Casa Gabriel) was not a boys home but a 24 hour, 7 day a week leadership training program. The high school aged boys going through the program just happen to live on site.

In the main dining room, 6 or 7 guys were crouched over their homework as a tutor helped them with the basics. A few other guys were in the kitchen doing the morning dishes as part of their every 'serving list'. They looked up at us and smiled, waved, shot a few thumbs up as we returned the greetings. These guys were great. Rough and street worn, they carried with them stories of abuse, gang involvement and a drug lifestyle. But they had a love for the Lord and an authenticity that captured our hearts.

The director said that they were unashamed of their faith in Christ. They shared that faith with everyone. Literally! One of the boys was given the opportunity to have dinner with the new President of Ecuador. He shared the truth that Jesus Christ died for even him and that by believing, the President could have eternal life. When the boy asked if the President would like to receive Christ as his Savior, the President politely mentioned that he went to the Catholic church.

We shared Makenzie's story. They shared Bible verses with us that were encouraging and loving. Before we arrived last week, Brad sent a list of the boys with their shoe preference. Nathan and I spent a morning buying them and yesterday, we handed them out. They were so excited. Many of them had never had a new pair of shoes before.

But the power of our visit was not in the matching the style and size of the shoes to the boys at Casa G. The power of today was not in seeing that the boys had responsibilities in the house and that they loved on each other. The power of the experience was hearing our stories; ours about Makenzie and theirs about themselves. Both our family and their "family" understood that whether we are in the states speaking English or here in Ecuador speaking Spanish, that God was the one who moved and breathed in our very lives. God was the one who, for whatever reason, allows tragedy, desperation and loss to be woven into the pattern of our life's tapestry.

Hearing Jose Luis's faith story of living on the streets and God's presence and provision during that time left us in stunned silence. Hearing how the staff is sold out to following Jesus in teaching servant leadership to this group of boys who have never been mentored by anyone was awe inspiring.

Our day ended by visiting Youth World's camp called El Refugio. "The Refuge" is a place where people can get away from the city and spend time with the Lord at this sprawling, 300 acre forest retreat center. Programming for groups and kids, challenge courses and a wonderful tree-house give glory and honor to the Lord through this outdoor ministry.

During past mission trips, it was about this day, day 4, that I was broken enough to want to go back to the states, sell everything I had and join whatever God was doing wherever that may be. This trip, I sense a different "calling" if one were to use that term. A call to partnership. A call to foundational involvement. Is it financial? I ain't got much. Prayer? That's sort of a given. I'm not sure what but I'll keep watching for those subtle whispers in which God takes such delight and calls me into tomorrow.

Ecuador- Day 5: Kellie's Perspective

November 26

(The following is from Kellie's Facebook perspective of our day 5 in Quito)

Quito, Ecuador Day 5. Each day we become more overwhelmed at the blessings that the Lord has given us on this trip. This day was filled to the brim. So much so that when we got in the car at each spot, we were speechless.

The main part of the day was at a Compassion International site called Carmin Bajo. Our drive there was across dirt roads amidst one of the very poorest sections of housing in Quito. I could tell from the looks on Nathan and Maddie's faces they were stunned that people could live in such extreme poverty. Many of the women are single moms and there are some single fathers. Alcoholism is prevalent as well as other substance abuse. Children are on their own most of the time. The school that we went to is called Alliance Academy and within it are kids sponsored through

Compassion International. We have a compassion child in the Dominican Republic that we have sponsored for the past 8 years so this was wonderful to be a part of even though we are in Ecuador.

There are 130 children in the school and when they come they receive one full meal a day. It typically

"90% of the children eat one meal a day"

consists of a meat and two starches. Potatoes and rice. This is so they can stay full. For 90% of them, this is the only meal they receive. After the weekend, the children are so enthusiastic about coming back to school. Obviously, the food is a big factor in that enthusiasm. For us, it was a convicting moment to realize how we take for granted being able to get fast food, go to the grocery store (where all the shelves are stocked) anytime. It gives me a whole new perspective on truly being hungry. We were honored to be included in serving the meal to students. There were three different age groups that we served. Tuna soup and then a plate of rice, potatoes and a very small piece of chicken and then a glass of strawberry juice.

When we arrived, the pastor's wife (Alliance Church; associated with the school) gave us a tour of the school. It certainly wouldn't pass any inspection in the United States, but for these people sitting on the side of the hill, it is a mansion. Each classroom greeted us with a Spanish expression of love and a very loud "Buenos Dias!"

The children were beautiful. If you don't know anything about what Compassion does, they provide medical help with shots and a doctor is provided to the specific area, food, clothing and other assistance through the sponsorship of each child. Most of their dollars come from North America.

What touched me to the core, was a moment in the kitchen when Sandy shared with the ladies working in the kitchen (they each had their own story and are members at the Alliance Church). Sandy told them who we were and why we were in Ecuador and all about Makenzie. There wasn't a moments hesitation with these women. They expressed their love to us through hugs and words of scripture and truth poured out of them. How could they do this when they didn't know Makenzie except for her picture and story? Jesus lives in them. In so many ways I was convicted on my lack of spiritual fervor. They spoke of how Makenzie is now experiencing roads of gold in heaven and how she would not want to be back here. They spoke of her life as if they knew her and that God has her right where He wants her.

For those of you who know me, that is the one thing I have "heard" consistently from the Lord. "I have Makenzie right where I have always wanted her, Kellie." I was shocked. How could I think that I have so much more than these people? They have what is important. Christ. Don't get me wrong, I have Christ in my heart. But, I saw they are living Christ out daily in their lives. They have so little but yet they have so much. The children there left an imprint on my heart. They all said words of thanks and "Chow!" to us when we left. We walked back up the hill; a mixture of cobblestone and earth that easily gave way under the treading of our feet to the car knowing that our lives had been changed.

One small note. In one of the classrooms was a new wood floor that they were all so proud of. The other floors are all cold concrete. In that classroom all the children had on slippers. Their shoes were neatly lined up outside the door. Since most of their shoes are pretty tattered and frankly would ruin the floor, that is the reason for the slippers. That was one of the needs. Slippers. Funny that we came here to give out shoes from Makenzie's project. I thought to myself, "you are so funny, Lord." So, from the offering at Lutheran South Academy in Houston, we were able to give 130 pairs of slippers to these children. Again, I was struck at how Makenzie would have rejoiced in doing this. Again, I was hit with a flood of tears at how my baby would have loved being here and why in the world are we here and not her. She was so much better at this than me. A torrent of anger

hit me as well about the
accident and then I am
reminded that God calls me to
forgive. Forgive the driver,

> *"God calls us me to forgive"*

forgive the situation and know that God has a bigger plan
with it all to bring others to Him. A true knowledge of
Him. It's what God wants me to do and what Makenzie
would have begged me to do.

After Carmin Bojo, we went back to Casa Gabriel. There
were a number of boys who were at school the day before
that we didn't get to give shoes to so we were able to do this
as well as bless them in another way. God provided
through a family at LSA (you know who you are) with a
cash gift to use in whatever way the Lord led us. At the
home, there is is no working stove and oven. There is one
there that barely works as an oven. Some of the boys have
taken on baking and know that they are good at it. They
make all the bread for the home (14 boys currently) and are
thinking about a micro -business where they can bake.

When we asked the amount needed to buy a new industrial oven/stove it was exactly what was given to us. When we put the money in the envelope for them, we realized all the bills had M.R.S. written on them...Makenzie Rebekah Stocker. Okay, Makenzie loved to eat. She also loved bread. The two things clicked and it was just obvious that this was provided for this moment. Way cool. Sorry this is so long today, I just had to get all my thoughts out about Day 5 in Quito. We came into this blind and now come out realizing that God is in control of all things. Our eyes have been opened to so much more. We knew this would happen but I don't think we were quite prepared for all the emotions. God is good. If you stumbled upon this, don't imagine for one moment that God doesn't love you. He does. He created us all with a purpose. No matter what is going on in your life, He desires for you to turn to Him, put your old ways and old life in the past, confess your sins, don't hang on to them and live for Him.

Ecuador- Looking Back

December 1

(Our family thoughts of experiencing God in Ecuador)

<u>Todd</u>: "You can't enter another culture, even for a brief moment, without being changed in someway. Sometimes the change happens as your heart is softened by the smile of a little child wearing tattered shoes. Sometimes the change happens as your eyes are opened to the desperate needs of people outside of your life's borders. Sometimes the change happens as you realize that God was already working in that foreign place and you simply joined Him in His efforts. Through our experience in Ecuador this past week, our family was changed in these ways and more."

<u>Kellie</u>: " I have the personality of a planner. These past few months, I've planned out the trip to Ecuador, coordinated chapels at LSA, taken care of all the shoes collected and prayed that the Lord would use us to serve as He saw fit.

Now, as we return to Minnesota, I find myself sad that this part of our journey has ended. This means I truly have to face the reality that Makenzie is gone from this Earth. A torrent of "whys?" come to mind after being in Houston but then I am reminded that the Lord has Makenzie in His embrace and presence. As a Mom, I have prayed that that is where my children would be; in fellowship with the Lord, knowing Him as their Savior.

Finishing the project that Makenzie began was a tremendous joy; heightened by the fact that we did it as a family. I can't help but hear her laughter in my mind at the things we did. Including finishing out the trip in Houston as we went to church and at lunch with all her friends. A "you did what?" crossed my mind but then I know that those friends and our family have a special bond. We probably always will. Because of Makenzie. Because of Christ.

I realize that by planning and being with her friends, I was keeping a bit of Makenzie alive so to speak. Now that we finished, I feel sad, because I don't want to go to the next thing in life without her. Again, I am nudged by the Lord. He says, He will be my strength and my guide. And as I am confronted with the fact the I face more days without her, I am comforted as well by our Lord's love and grace. The same love and grace I was able to show to the people of Ecuador."

Nathan: "I was fascinated by the fact that we Americans have the thought that "I'm going to serve you because that's what good people do." God doesn't want us to just serve and serve and serve to be sympathetic and think that we get brownie points for it. Give, give, give. No, we are to give AND receive. Be blessed. I was surprised to arrive in Quito, and experience a taste of what we came to dish out. The people there, were not only there to be served by us,

"God wants us to give and receive"

but also to return the serving. Absolutely fascinating. I think that we Americans have the mindset of "I'm here for you," or "No, no, I insist you take this." And sometimes that is a good thing. But we as humans need to receive, as well as give."

Maddie: "Today is the last day in Quito and boy has it been a wonderful week. I have experienced a lot of emotional things this past week. I am very thankful that I have a home and food and shelter and people that care for me like my mom and dad. Every day, we did something new that just warmed my heart and it made me say every time "Wow, I wish Kenzie was here!!" Most people I saw on the streets were mostly little kids trying to earn money for their familia. In America, only parents have to work. Ecuador was a very good trip and it's an awesome privilege for me to have a family."

(Todd's last thought): After returning from a mission trip that Makenzie and I took together, she told me, "After working with those people; after helping them and building them their house, I think they blessed me more that I blessed them."

If you're hesitant to step outside your borders and crossover to a distant land, remember that God is already there. You will be joining Him in His work of finding and saving people who are lost and you'll never be the same again.

18th Birthday
Pg. 195

Maddie, Makenzie
and Nathan

Maddie, Kellie, Todd,
Makenzie and Nathan

Makenzie and Me
performing in the
Nutcracker, '08
Pg. 121

Makenzie
goofing around

Makenzie's New Years Resolutions, '08
Pg. 139

Makenzie's Prom with
friend, Alex Baltes, 5/09
Pg. 201

Girlfriends:
Katie Davis, Nancy Wukasch,
Emilie Finke, and
Makenzie Stocker at prom '09
("Sneak Attacks" by Katie, pg 27)

Pictures from the last photo shoot, the night of the car accident

Makenzie and Caitlin Cannon, friend, dance partner and photographer who took the last photo's of Makenzie

The last picture of Makenzie alive - 8:03, pm. 5 minutes before the accident

One of the last pictures of Makenzie. The clock behind her reads 8:00, 8 minutes before the accident

Stopped at the intersection, Makenzie's friend, Caitlin, took this shot. The middle cloud looks like an open door. The cloud on the right looks like an open hand - palm up. 3 seconds after this shot was taken, they took a left, went through the intersection and Makenzie was killed, instantly as their car was broadsided by a truck. 8:08 pm, June 3, 2009

The car in which Makenzie was a passenger

A tree planted in Makenzie's memory at Mark and Lisa Baltes' cabin
Pg. 38

Makenzie's handprint on my windshield. I didn't wash it off for 18 months
Pg. 40

Girls in Kenya heard about Makenzie and began a worship dance troop which travels to churches performing for the Lord
Pg. 223

Soles for Souls
November 18 – December 1

LUTHERAN SOUTH ACADEMY
HERANSOUTH.ORG

"YOU TURNED MY MOURNING INTO DANCING"
(PSALM 30)
FINISHING WHAT MAKENZIE STARTED
FOR OUR PRAYER REQUESTS AND UPDATES, GO TO
WWW.TODDSTOCKER.WORDPRESS.COM

Makenzie never delivered the 2200 pairs of shoes she collected for Ecuador. Our family went there to finish what she started in Nov. '09
Pg. 87

Maddie and Nathan with Ecuadorian girl at The Dump's daycare center Pg. 93

Happy girl wearing her new shoes and carrying her old ones

Todd and Kellie putting new shoes on the children of Quito, Ecuador

Kellie, Maddie, Makenzie, Todd, and Nathan Stocker.
The last picture of us together, Easter weekend, 2009
Pg. 186

"You turned my mourning into dancing. You clothed me with joy. I will thank You forever."
Psalm 30

The Dance of Your Life - The Nutcracker

December 5

As I drive the streets of my Facebook friends' posts and tags and farkles (whatever those are!?), I am reminded that this is Nutcracker season for Makenzie's Ballet Company. (This would've been her last one with the dance family that she grew to love). For me, my mind sparkles with the memories of sharing that experience with her on stage.

Below is an article I wrote for the magazine Connect Quarterly a few years back, about dancing with my graceful daughter who now dances with Jesus:

"I cannot believe that I am publicly going to admit this, but ... this year, I am a ballerina. Ok, technically, a male ballerina is called a Cavalier but whatever the title, I'm making a sacrifice. Let me explain.

My daughter, Makenzie, is the real ballerina and every year, her company performs Tchaikovsky's The Nutcracker. If you have a child in this performance, you know that every level of dance is involved in the production. From little kids through older adults, every age group is on stage!

In The Nutcracker, one of the opening scenes involves adults at a Christmas Eve party at the Baron and Baroness Stahlbaum's home. This scene requires adults to play the roles of partygoers and enjoy watching children dance, receive gifts and be entertained. With a shortage of talented adults, the casting representative became desperate and called me.

"Pastor Todd, would you play a part in your daughter's Nutcracker performance?" When I thought about donning tights and 'jazz shoes,' visions of a bad Mel Brooks movie popped into my head.

Nevertheless, in a weak moment, I said yes. Yes, I will stumble around on stage, pretending I had grace. Yes, I will endure being the target of degrading jokes at work from those who do not understand the arts, but I don't care.

I am doing this first for my daughter and secondly for me. You see, it is one thing to watch her dance from an anonymous chair in the back of a dark balcony. It's quite another to be on stage with her, trading glances and smiles, dancing together, just the two of us in front of thousands.

Many of you reading this have the impression that God is not on your stage. That He is only watching from a distance as you try to find your next dance move. As you stumble from one broken relationship to another disappointment, you wonder if God even bought a ticket to your show.
Matthew 1:23 says,

"The virgin will be with child and will give birth to a son, and they will call him Immanuel"–which means, "God with us."

Did you catch that? God is with you! Not just in the peaceful, fun times but especially in the dark, confusing times. He is on the stage of your life! Directing, producing, and performing with you in your 'Nutcracker'. No matter what you think, no matter what you believe, no matter what you have experienced or endured, God is

with you. He is Immanuel and He knows that the performance is not easy. He knows that sometimes your life is tough and the steps to the dance seem to get more and more difficult. But there is not a moment of your dance from which He is absent! Even when you think you don't want Him involved, He is there.
Psalm 139:7 says,

> "Where can I go from your Spirit? Where can I flee from your presence?"

God being with you is what Christmas is about. You are not dancing alone! The Christmas celebration centers on Jesus coming to earth to be with us, from the first act to the drop of the final curtain, Jesus is with you.

So dance your heart out! Wear tights if you want to. Because your Immanuel, Jesus Christ, is with you, disciplining your sinful steps and loving you above it all! By the way, if you are at one of the 14 performances of the Nutcracker in November and December, look for my daughter. She will be the graceful one with her proud dad only a whispers distance away.

Is It Over?

December 5

It's early morning and I just lit a fire. I'm hoping that it's warmth will cut the icy chill that invades our snow sacked home. Framed by only four red stockings, I'm watching the flames dance sporadically on the log that is their stage. Our Christmas tree crowds some of my view but icicles, bulbs and ornaments are reflecting the glow from the hearth. A lone candy cane dangles at the end of one branch, inviting me to sneak it away and the steam from my morning coffee drifts up into nowhere.

This is our home's Christmas scene. It is the perfect scene and should cause my love for the season to overwhelm me. Except, it doesn't.

Normally, I begin playing Christmas music in October. Normally, I browse the aisles of Christmas TV specials, giggling like a school-kid. But this year is not normal. It is one of the many "firsts" that we're experiencing without

Makenzie. And it is the first time in my living memory that I've wanted it all to be over.

> "Jesus is the reason for the season"

I have fought the Scroog-ian urge to declare "Bah-Hum Bug" because I don't feel that negatively about it all. Yes, I am looking forward to our church's Christmas Concert and the "Holidazzle Parade" in frigid Minneapolis, but to say that I'm overjoyed that its Christmas is a stretch. Why? Because, as her dad, I loved seeing Makenzie love at Christmastime. I enjoyed seeing her dance her heart out at the Nutcracker and being with her on her stage. I smiled as I watched her love on all the little ballerina's, hug total strangers, and declare that this was the best time of year! I will miss the rolling of her friends' eyes when the phrase "Jesus is the reason for the season" floats off her lips. I will miss seeing her hug her brother and sister on Christmas morning and tell them she loves them. I will especially miss her draping her arms around my neck and softly tell me, "I'm so glad you're my Daddy! I love you!"

The fire is dying down. My coffee is now cold and my day's schedule is calling for me. I don't want to leave this moment but I also don't want to stay in it any longer. Our first Christmas without Makenzie. Now I know how it feels.

The Christmas Prayer

December 14

As a pastor, the Christmas season brought extra work loads, meetings and message preps. Peel off my griping and complaining, however, and you'll find my heart overjoyed and humbled at being one of the many to lead God's people in celebrating the birthday of our King. The shepherds, the angels, the road-trip to Bethlehem. It is all so magical; even to your pastor.

For me, I love the "feel" of the worship services. The words "Joyful," "Adore," and "Merry" drip from everyones lips as the candle light cuts through the darkness of the evening. The worship story unfolds so smoothly until that one part of the service that seems to throw a wet blanket on the whole party. The Prayers. Before you cast the heretical stone, let me explain. Look through any worship folder and eventually you see this part of the prayers announced that previously made my skin crawl. Maybe as an insert; maybe as a simple statement; it is the prayer for those "who have lost loved ones."

I have so many theological complaints about the statement itself (Are they really lost? Do I have the power to loose them? etc. etc. blah. blah. blah). But reminding the congregation that this Christmas will be different from all others; that someone who lived in your life for many (or a few) years is not going to be around; that the person who lit up your heart and everyone else's was gone, forever; this never seemed to be on my worship party event list. One year, I was so disgusted with this dam that was set up in the river of our praise that I jumped over it all together. (Come to think of it, I remember the pianist scrambling to the keyboard as I suddenly announced the final hymn... ah, good times).

This year, I have a different take on those prayers. I still wish we wouldn't point out the obvious fact that Makenzie will not be with our family this year (or any others), but I celebrate that she is eating birthday cake with our King Jesus. I celebrate the truth that heaven is real and that I will be there with Makenzie to praise Him in person. I look forward to holding up candles with her and secretly dripping wax on the wings of the angel Michael. I can't wait to harmonize with her as we belt out "Joyful, Joyful We Adore Thee!" to the One who made heaven possible for a sinner like me.

Our family has not lost Makenzie, this Christmas. We all know exactly where she is. But as we weep quietly in the back of the bough draped church, we will thank God for the past 18 times that we celebrated Christmas with our oldest daughter. Merry Christmas, Makenzie; Merry Christmas.

Our Family Christmas Book

December 16

Our mailbox is giving birth daily to Christmas cards, letters and notes that our family and friends send this time of year. For many of them, this is the only time that we hear their past years story or see that little Johnny grew 3 inches. (Shocking!).

Writing our family Christmas letter and taking our family Christmas picture was always fun for us. Maddie would squirm, Nathan would sport a cheesy smile and Makenzie would try to get them to "look nice." Sometimes, we were in a park, sometimes, in our home, but every year's picture captured the joy that we shared as a family ... all 5 of us. Then, after the tree was down and the decorations were put away, Kellie would take that year's Christmas letter/picture, put it in a Hallmark book and write down the memories that defined the season. It was always a joy to flip back through those pages; watching how God grew our family, year after year, remember the church services in which I played a part and reminisce about the gifts that the kids ripped into on Christmas morning. That Christmas book had become part of our family's seasonal experience.

When Makenzie died, we moved. During the packing process, I discovered our beloved Christmas book at the bottom of a water soaked bin in the back of our garage. Pages, now mush, slopped on the floor as I pinched it's corner and lifted it out of the stagnant water. The words "Our Family Christmas" were barely legible on the cover of the book that was now overrun by black mold. It's yellowed pages were streaked with the unreadable ink that once held words that were our memories. Another loss and another reminder that our family was being forced to start over. I had to let it go.

If the book had survived, the page titled "Christmas, 2009" would have been empty, anyway. When death strikes your family in such a profound way, there are certain traditions, practices and habits that you put to the side; simply because you can't go through the pretension that you are having a good time. As a result, you probably won't get a Christmas card/picture from us in

> "When death strikes, many things are put to the side"

the mail this year. We just haven't brought ourselves to take one without Makenzie. But we want you to know that while we have "Makenzie Moments" throughout the day, we are doing ok. Our joy is a bit tarnished; our happiness is not as bright, but the love of God that is displayed to us through our family and friends brings us closer to the manger of our Lord.

Keep sending your cards. Keep stuffing our mailbox. 'Cause while we can't respond, we love them ... and we love you.

Christmas Nostalgia

December 23

They say that the "first-without" Christmas is difficult; when you've had someone you love die during the previous months. For me, the word "difficult" doesn't describe how I am experiencing my Christmas. Honestly, I couldn't come up with a word because the emotions that dance around me are usually two bed-fellows that you'd never put together. Joy and Grief, Fullness and Loss. They flood me when I think about Makenzie.

This Christmas has been no different from any other day since June 3rd. I have Makenzie Moments – the reminders that she is gone – and it makes me sad. I remember her snorty laugh and it makes me smile. I remember her beauty, charm, and joy and it makes me proud. I remember our last few Christmases with her and it makes me nostalgic.

Maybe that is the word that describes the Christmas season for me. Nostalgic. (You can tell I am a processing writer). Anyway ... nostalgic. It is a wistful desire to return in thought or in fact to a former time in one's life (thank you, dictionary.com). But in many ways, that is what I'd like to do; return to a time when Makenzie was alive. Those who know her would echo me. I'd like to be standing with Kellie on stage again at the Nutcracker, watching our daughter wow the crowd as she spun without effort on the tip of her toe. I'd like to relive the sleepy Christmas morning as all 5 of us sunk into our overstuffed couch, open presents in our 'jami's and hear Makenzie's heavy sigh as she bit into one of Kellie's scones. I'd like to re-experience the undeserved, out-of-the-blue hugs that Kenzie would give me and hear her say again, "I love you, Daddy."

I wonder if that is how Mary felt at the foot of the cross of her son, her Savior, Jesus. Nostalgic ... wanting to return to a time and place where simply shepherds and learned wise men bent their knee to worship her little boy. I guess, Mary and I have something in common.

"But Mary treasured up all these things and pondered them in her heart."
Luke 2:19

The Rung in Front of Me

December 28

I don't have a fear of heights as some do. Sure, standing two feet away from a certain death, 100 foot drop into Arizona's Grand Canyon makes my knees mushy, but overall, I can now scale a tall ladder with the best of em. I conquered that fear a few Christmases ago when the empty peak of our 25 foot home entry cried out for a six foot wide wreath. Normally, I'd scale the back of the house and lower the lighted monstrosity into place, but this home sported steep angles. So I stationed a ladder at the base of the front entry, leaned it against the wall and stood there... looking up at what seemed to be miles high. Strapping the mammoth wreath to my back and planting my foot on the bottom rung, I rehearsed in my mind, "Don't look down ... Don't look down." Four rungs up, I was frozen; staring at the concrete only 3 feet below and praying my wife wouldn't see me hugging the ladder like a lover. "What a wimp," I thought of myself. I began to muster up the guts enough,

"Just one step" not to look up at the top or bottom of the ladder, but simply at the rung in front of me. My feet thawed and I took another step up. The rung in front of me I thought again. "One foot up ... the rung in front of me". Like Dorie's chant, "Just keep swimming ... Just keep swimming," the phrase "the rung in front of me" kept me moving on with the task at hand. Soon I was scampering up and down the ladder like a squirrel on a tree, finishing my husbandly duty of 'Christmas-izing' my home

God gave me the encouragement to look at the rung in front of me as I climb my ladder of grief. At times, I am frozen with hurt. At times, I am clinging to His Cross with fear. But mostly, I am looking at this day, this hour, this moment as the rung in front of me.

"Do not worry about tomorrow; tomorrow will worry about itself. Each day has enough trouble of it's own."
Matthew 6:34

I Want to Witness a Miracle

January 1

Resolutions. Dreams. Hopes. Each year, our family spends a few minutes after the proverbial "ball drop" to write these down as we close our eyes on the past 12 months. Once written, our musings hibernate in an envelope until the next December. Then, they are opened and read. Some years, our thoughts are about being a better student. Other years, they reflect a desire to have, as my wife describes, a "weight change." (This time around, I fulfilled that one but not the kind of change for which she was hoping).

We spent a few moments this evening, (nay ... morning), reading last years dreams ... from all five of us, saving Makenzie's till the end. For this past year, 2009, her resolutions were, in ascending order:

☑ *Love, be loved, love others and find love!*

☑ *Live above the noise and not make this year regrettable.*

☑ *Not take life for granted ... and show it.*

☑ *Learn a song on the guitar.*

☑ *Become more observant of everything around me.*

☑ *Become a better dancer."*

(And number one on her list for this past year) ...

☑ *I want to witness a miracle.*

Truthfully, every breath that fills our lungs, every moment through which our hearts beat, every thought, word and action that defines us – shapes us – are miracles because they are all undeserved. But my Makenzie's desire to witness a miracle that year was fulfilled in a way that none could fathom. The miracle that she witnessed was being face to face with the God who created her. She witnessed the miracle of her life being redeemed and her purpose being completed. She witnessed the miracle of Jesus' arms wrapping around her and taking her home to be with Him forever.

May we all witness a miracle this year from our Lord who is the God of the miraculous.

Wish You Were Here

January 16

The phrase, "Wish You Were Here," has sarcasm as it's nameplate. I used the phrase often while basking in the Houston warmth and talking to my Minnesota buddy, Scott, in February's past. But rarely did I utter the words without a sense of dig... of scoffing ... of tongue in cheek.

I find myself thinking phrase consistently, now. 'I wish Makenzie were here'. However, there is no hint of humor; not a shadow of play. I simply, truly, desperately wish Makenzie were here.

It's been 7 months since God took Makenzie home and our new normal lives have gone on. Ironically, the great things that are happening in and to our family are coupled with reminders that one is missing. I don't know how long it lasts — others may know — but my gut reactions when something interesting takes place is to think, "I can hardly wait to tell Makenzie," followed by, "I wish you were here."

"Makenzie! On the same day that Nathan's braces came off, Maddie's went on. (I wish you could see them). Kellie may be speaking to a large group of high school students. (I wish you could hear her). We are going sledding today on your favorite hill. (I wish you could come)."

> " *I can hardly wait to see Makenzie again* "

The public mourning is now private but no less painful. Our life is good up here in the north country. But, selfishly, I still wish you were here.

An Emotional Agnostic

January 26

Emotionally, I'd be a good agnostic (one who believes there's a God but doesn't believe He's involved in everyday life). Like David in the Psalms, I cry out, "Where are you God? Have you abandon me? Are you unaware of the emptiness that swallows my ability to get out of bed? Were you sleeping when the car rolled through the intersection, was broadsided and became the death chamber for Makenzie? Where are you God?"

But what I've re-learned through Makenzie's life/death/life is that those times of emotional sorrow that still ambush moments in my day are also mental reminders that God is not distant. He is not a philosophy or a life-path but a personal Being who knows what it's like to loose a child. He reminds me that even though there are times when I feel that He's not all that smart, He knows what He's doing.

At Makenzie's Celebration Service, the Pastor said, "To God, this was no accident." In other words, even the tragedy that took my daughter was known, and dare I say it, planned by God to show a greater purpose, my faith in God is not based on feelings but facts. Sound cliche? To me, it does. But it's a cliche that I'll think about. It calms my emotions, dulls my pain and gives me the moment-by-moment strength that keeps me from becoming an emotional agnostic.

"I cried out to the Lord in my distress and groaned. Has He forgotten to be merciful? But then I remembered what He's done in the past. Your ways are perfect, O God."
(from Psalm 77)

Rejecting the EITHER; Accepting the OR.

January 28

Life gets tough. Expectations go unmet and frustration rumbles through our emotions like thunder from a distant storm.

I remember a time in recent years that church work felt like that for me. We moved across the country, leaving family and friends and a church community that I dearly loved, to take on another ministry challenge. After several years in my new position, I was struggling to see why God allowed the stress that was affecting my faith, my family and my sanity.

Finally, I sat down with a Pastor/friend of mine and dribbled my irritation all over his desk. He leaned forward, looked me dead in the eye and simply said, "EITHER, God has made a terrible mistake OR He has you here for a purpose." EITHER ... OR.

Now, I know the character of God. I know that He isn't surprised by anything

> "God is not surprised by anything"

and that He orchestrates and weaves my life story into a saga that is uniquely mine. Based on that truth, I had to reject the EITHER and accept the OR. God knows what He is doing. He isn't surprised by anything and He doesn't make mistakes.

Fast forward (or reverse) to June 3rd of last year. God knew (even before she was born) that Makenzie would be on a photo shoot with her dance friends that night. He knew that at 8:06pm, they would get into the car and start their journey home. He knew that the beautiful sunset He painted on the canvas of the sky, would be Makenzie's last on this earth. He knew that at 8:08pm, at a horrible intersection in Houston, that their car and a truck would violently meet, taking Makenzie's life and changing countless others.

God did not stand on the corner, witness the accident and say, "WHOA! I didn't see that coming." (That's the EITHER, which I have rejected). Somehow, in some way, for some reason, my precious Lord scripted that scene to fit within the greater play.

Right now, I see glimpses of purpose; shadows of His plan. And as the whole thing unfolds I will reject the EITHER and accept the OR.

"I don't think the way you think.
The way you work isn't the way I work. God's Decree."
Isaiah 55:8

Pew Diving - by Katie Davis

January 29

One of Makenzie's dear friends, Katie Davis, started a blog to tell stories about their school life together. A while back, she noted a funny story that I thought you could take with you as you go to Worship this weekend. Enjoy ...

"Our Sophomore year, our music teacher took us to his church to rehearse before a concert. This was always an exciting day because we would get sandwiches delivered to us in a box. Anyway, while on our break Kenzie and I created a new form of entertainment. We called it "Pew diving". (When I think about this now, I think this was a little disrespectful). But we would take a running leap and slide down the pew on our stomachs and see who could get farther. Sometimes our shirts would slide up a little bit and we would get rubbed and turn red and end up with a bruise. Anyway, our teacher ruined our fun after about 10 mins and made us stop. But you can just imagine Kenzie and I taking running leaps into the pews and laughing at the top of our lungs. Sadly, I don't have any pictures of us doing this."

Stop the Mail

February 1

Another one came in the mail recently. It had her name on it; printed in collegiate lettering. The opening line ... "Makenzie! You've been invited to apply to (insert college name). You can pursue your dreams at (college name) and all it takes is simply to fill out the enclosed application." Arg.

Another reminder. Another disappointment. Another mnemonic telling me that I won't be helping her fill out the application as other moms and dads have been doing the past few months. There will be a college that will not experience Makenzie's joy; her laugh; her excitement for the Lord, dance and life! There will be new students that won't hear Makenzie greet them with a "I'm new here! Just like you! Wanna be friends?" And I feel badly for them.

Normally I look forward to getting the mail. Now, not so much. Next year, they will stop. Her name will drop from their lists and I will be relieved not to get those pieces of postage. Funny. It's the simple daily things that make me realize the complexity of loss.

White as Snow

February 2

There are benefits to living in this part of God's country: Ice fishing, Lutefisk and dead car batteries. For my warm weather dwellers, this experience is called "Minnesota Winter." Casting my sarcasm into a snowdrift, I do enjoy the crisp, early mornings cut through by the warmth of my fire-warmed hearth.

> *"My sins are made white as snow"*

This morning, snow is dancing down from the heavens and covering that which had been ugly. The gray slush that lies by the side of the roads; the frozen muck that clings to the undercarriage of my car; the evidence of my dog's empty bladder in a shoveled area just off the deck; all of it covered by the light dusting of simple flakes.

Reminds me of the verse,

"Come now, let us reason together," says the LORD. "Though your sins are like scarlet, they shall be as white as snow."
Isaiah 1:18

That, which is in me, has been covered up by the snow of God's forgiveness. The dirt that exposed itself out of the anger of our families loss, has been blanketed by the robe of Christ. I feel forgiven today. I feel loved today. I feel white as snow.

Not Taken For Granted

February 8

Superbowl. Big deal. My Vikings weren't playing and even if they were, I'm not sure I would've given up yesterday's events to watch the game; even the commercials. While Nathan was working at the local chalet at the ski-slopes, Kellie persuaded (or was that forced) Maddie and I to go skiing for the first time this year. Out on the snow blanketed hills, I taught Maddie all I knew about skiing (which amounted to snowplowing and how to get up after you fall). She loved it. And because of that, I loved it. And because of that, Kellie loved it. And because of that, Nathan said, "I told you so."

Zooming down the slopes diverted my musing from the past months to the present moment. All four of us, having fun together; and not thinking about our one who was not there. In those hours of frozen joy, I refreshed my commitment not to take the remainder of my family for granted. I fixed a short lens over my thoughts and saw

Kellie, Maddie, Nathan and me for what we are; a family who enjoys hanging around each other and loves each other. We are all we got. And I'm not going to take another moment with them for granted.

That Reminds Me

February 11

Makenzie is one of my two daughters. She is not here. She is in my future; taken from my today and grafted into my tomorrow. I miss her like an asthmatic misses a full breath of air. I want her back but know that will never be. I have videos, pictures; written remembrances from friends and occasional reminders from simple events and everyday people; like Courtney.

> *"Makenzie is not in my past, but my future"*

Courtney helped us at the bank yesterday. Cute; blonde; young and full of life (like Makenzie). Pictures of her friends and family hung from the sterile gray fabric that lined her well-lit cubical. Sitting on her desk was a 3×5 picture of her newlywed husband staring out over the words I LOVE YOU, etched into the bottom of the frame. Suddenly, I likened Courtney to Makenzie. In a moment, I played out Makenzie's never-to-be wedding in my mind. I pictured myself, meeting her at the bank to take her — Makenzie - to lunch. I thought about helping her and her life-companion make life decisions as they walked through ... life. Not to be.

Then, as my thoughts leaned back into the moment, I saw Courtney grasp her pen and write. Holding the utensil like a popsicle, the upper portion of her thumb pumped up and down with every jot and tittle. "Our daughter, Makenzie, writes just like that," I blurted. "Really? I thought I was the only one," she said casually. Kellie and I locked eyes, exchanged a smile and cried inside.

Moments like these keep us going and hold us back. They are little reminders that Makenzie is still ours but not within reach. They help us to utter three healing words, "That Reminds Me."

I'm Giving Up, 'Giving Up', For Lent.

February 17

I never really understood the idea of GIVING UP something for Lent. Several religious friends of mine would give up eating meat. Others would give up a certain beverage or snack. Still others would give up a hurtful habit only to pick it up again at the dawning of the post-Easter season. That's just didn't make sense. I tried giving up, but like other resolutions past, it didn't take long for me to sneak it back into my daily repertoire of vices, sins and ills. How defeating!

Now, instead of giving up, I take on during Lent. My thoughts aren't on stopping something secular, but adding something spiritual. For instance, several years ago, I began journaling— spending time with the Lenten bible verses and writing down my impressions, musings and applications. Other years I've added a different aspect of prayer. This year, I'm adding daily "Thanks You's" to my Lord because I have truck-loads for which to be grateful.

I'm thankful for the way He kept our family intact after That Day. I'm thankful for how He has taken us on a step by step journey and hasn't let our feet slip. I'm thankful that He gave me Heaven even when I asked for Hell. And, as the days wear on, I'm thankful that someday soon, I'll get to hug my oldest daughter again. All thanks to my God who sent Jesus to make it happen.

"...I'll show up and take care of you as I promised and bring you back home. I know what I'm doing. I have it all planned out—plans to take care of you, not abandon you, plans to give you the future you hope for."
Jeremiah 29:11, The Message Paraphrase.

Sacrifice

February 20

SACRIFICE. Isn't that what Lent is all about? Not the
sacrifice of cheap habits, vices or sins, but the glacial giving
of one's very earthly existence for the saving of others;
'saving' on a scale of life's ills to life's death.

My dear sister, Stephanie, sent this observation from her 4
year old daughter, Anna. Anna, a youngster, articulated
this deep theology through the words of a simple, preschool song:

*"There's a song Anna learned from preschool. It goes
"Why did God send Jesus to die? L-O-V-E, love that's
why!" But Anna has been singing it like this: "Why did
God send Kenzie to die? L-O-V-E, love that's why!" (I'm
not sure why she changed it; maybe because she
associates dying with Kenzie; who knows!)*

Anyway, I thought it was an interesting way to look at it...
God allowed this to happen because of His love. He

knows the plans for us and His plans are motivated out of "L-O-V-E, love that's why!" As I think

> *"God's plans are motivated from love"*

about this, it's hard to understand with my puny human brain – all I want to do is shake an accusing finger at Him for all of the hurt. God's "L-O-V-E, love that's why" is different than our human love (thank goodness!). God's love is a selfless love, a love that was passionately committed to the well-being of the other. The only way to fathom this "L-O-V-E, love that's why" is by looking at the cross of Christ - God being passionately committed to us. There are so many moments that I simply want to understand why Makenzie's unexpected death had to happen. But what I learned through my daughter's lyrical liberty on her preschool song has given me a momentary lift from the sorrow in my heart. God's plans for us are motivated out of His "L-O-V-E, love that's why." Enough said."

My Pen Pal

February 24

He found me by way of the Lutheran Witness article I
wrote this past January. I received a letter — yes, in the
mail! — from this man whose daughter was killed in similar
circumstances to Makenzie's death. He wrote of his
daughter's joy, the music in her soul and her eloquence with
words. I could sense anguish as each finger-stroke
transferred his heart to ink on a page.

He wrote, "We lost our 20 year old daughter, 35 years ago
and I think about her everyday."

35 years ago! This man is forty years my senior yet his
sorrow is as fresh today as it was in the past; one score and
fifteen! (...that would be '35').

Am I to look forward to that emptiness the rest of my days
on earth? Will I have to navigate, for my remaining
moments, those thoughts that cause me to momentarily

freeze-up? When (or if) I saunter around at 84 years, will my ache be satisfied or the glimpses be extinguished. I know the answer is no. My pen-pal confirms it.

Yet, it is settled that June 3rd is part of my story; not a bump in the road but a direction shift in the journey. Things are different. Life is different. Our family is different. But my Jesus is the same. And in His letter, He says all is well; Makenzie is with Him and I will see her again soon. Can't wait.

Jesus answered, "I tell you the truth, today you will be with me in paradise."
Luke 23:43

NUMBERS

March 3

The Makenzie Moments have lessened their frequency. The hurt that comes is diminished. "Time is the healer of all wounds," they say, but I've found that not all wounds heal. Some are constantly picked over making the sting of loss real again. The "picker" that comes to mind this morning struts around disguised as NUMBERS.

... 3 ...

The 3rd of March; of December; of August; it doesn't matter. It is the 3rd that marks the day that my precious Makenzie stepped out of this world and into eternity. As of this 3rd, it has been 9 months since the accident.

... 9 ...

9 months that the Lord stitched the fabric of Makenzie together in the safe place of her mother's womb. 9 months

of close connection and now 9 months separation to which the remaining 4 in our family have had to adjust.

... 4 ...

4 plates at the table instead of five. The 4 of us going to a movie; the 4 of us watching American Idol. It's only the 4 of us. I'm still getting use to just the 4 of us and I'm sensing that it will never feel complete. I love the 4 of us but still miss the 1.

... 1 ...

1 life having such an impact on so many. 1 person making others feel valued, worthy and loved. 1 person sacrificing reputation, popularity, status and comfort so that other's can know what it is to truly LIVE. That 1 is the One with whom Makenzie dances on streets of gold. His name is Jesus ... and He calms my NUMBERS.

The Crucible - Heating (1 of 7)

March 9

The Lord uses every experience we face to reveal something about ourselves. For His purpose, He uses difficulties to shape and form us into the people He wants us to be. Someone stated, "Character is formed in the crucible of adversity." Great line ... wish I'd penned it. Especially since it is the crucible with which I deal every day.

In the meantime, I am a refiner. Yes, I also don the hats of pastor, writer, and communicator but my daily work while on my healing sabbatical is refiner. I melt down miscellaneous gold and silver into little bars that then are shipped out to be remolded into the jewelry that we all wear. The whole process is, at its foundation, a process of recycling. It is a violent process. It is a heat-intensifying cycle and it is necessary to turn that which is not being used at its full potential into something beautiful, desirable and worth more than before the process began.

Join me, these next writings — as you have been — as we enter the Crucible.

"Consider it pure joy, my brothers, whenever you face trials
of many kinds."
James 1:2

The Crucible - Night Light (2 of 7)

March 10

We know the word Crucible by two common expressions:
First, the Crucible it is the container in which metals or
other materials are melted. Second, the Crucible is a
metaphor we use for hard experiences, trials and
difficulties. But there is a third ... a little known moniker
that illuminates an unexpected purpose of the Crucible.
The word itself, "Crucible," originally meant "night-light."

Yup — Night-light. If you have young-ins, the shining from
the night-light is muted by Sponge-Bob, Hello Kitty or
some other personification of a non-threatening-politically-
correct-run-on-biofuel object. If you harbor a decades-long
nyctophobia (fear of darkness), your night-light simply
glows green from a flat panel plugin. Whatever the
holding, the night-light's purpose is this: to pull back the
dark and reveal that which couldn't be seen otherwise.

Ironic, isn't it? The violent Crucible and the soothing Night-light are one in the same with two different purposes married together in a single bond. The loss of your job should cause you to tail spin (darkness). But God uses it to show you that He will provide all your needs (light). The crumbling of a relational bond should force the grip of depression to squeeze the life out of you (darkness). But God uses it to reassure you that He will never leave (light). The unexpected death of your daughter causes you to freeze up with despair, sadness and pain (darkness). But God uses it to show you that even in the Crucible, He is still in control (light).

The Crucible. The night-light for your purpose. The night-light for His Love. The harsh tool in the hands of a gentle Refiner. Welcome to the Crucible.

The Crucible - Protected (3 of 7)

March 14

The furnace sounds like a jet engine. It roars; it hisses, waiting to be fed; eager to consume anything that it is given. And it will. Linger too long in the furnace and even the Crucible meets a cruel end which enlightens an ironic purpose of the Crucible. Protection.

Without the Crucible, the metal is doomed. Left to fight the furnace on it's own, the silver and gold would be liquified into a useless pile of slag. But within the Crucible, the Refiner can control the amount and intensity of the heat that the metal experiences. Albeit a cruel and violent tool, the Crucible protects the metal from certain uselessness if not obliteration.

"What was intended for harm was provided for good"

Reminds me of Jonah. The bible said that the Lord provided a whale to swallow Jonah (Jonah 1:7). Without the whale, Jonah would have certainly drown. I don't think Jonah saw it that way but nevertheless, the truth that is revealed is this; that which was intended for harm ultimately was provided for good.

My humanness can't grasp that truth but the Holy Spirit within can. "No matter how difficult the Crucible of our loss has been, my Refiner is still in control. No matter how brutal, ruthless or slow, the Crucible is a agonizing gift that is melting, molding and making me into something that my Refiner can really use."

Welcome to the Crucible.

The Crucible - Defiant (4 of 7)

March 16

Because I'm human, I stand defiant against change. Knowing who's behind it all, I sometimes grab Him by the tie, pull Him towards me over the table, stare Him right in the eye and mumble, "Go ahead and try to change me!" He simply smiles, puts on His goggles and heat shield, and lowers me into the Crucible.

From inside, I still stand straight, like a fork; prongs pointing skyward; trying to show that I'm not going to melt. Even as my Savior Refiner is setting me gently into the roar of the blazing furnace, I stand in defiance against the heat; refusing to bend; refusing to change; refusing to give in.

I am arrogant; I am foolish.

If you were to watch me in the Crucible, you would see me start to sweat. You would see my prongs begin to curl. You would see me — still defiant — tilt to one side and then disappear beneath the rim of the Crucible.

I am melted; I am undone. And my Savior Refiner is still in control.

Eventually, every piece of metal that enters the Crucible, is subject to this process. Once useful, then useless, then defiant, then changed, then useful again. It is a good process yet harsh. It is one that my humanness does not desire nor seek out. Yet, it is the only way.

Welcome to the Crucible.

> "Going a little ahead, Jesus fell on his face, praying, 'My Father, if there is any way, get me out of this! But please, not what I want. You, what do you want?'"
>
> Matthew 26:39

The Crucible - Scars (5 of 7)

March 18

All of us who are refiners, bear scars. They are scars that tell stories of a dropped mold, a misplaced stir rod or a hand too close to the fire. As I pen this, I am looking at a scar on my right wrist; one that I incurred as I lifted a heavy Crucible out of the furnace, exposing my skin to it's non-forgiving heat.

> *"My Savior Refiner transforms me into something new"*

But that's what it takes to be a refiner; to work with the defiant metal; to handle the Crucible; to make something good again. It takes sacrifice.

All refiners bear scars.

I am looking once again at my scar. But this time, I see it in light of my Savior Refiner, who bore scars, who willingly endured the Crucible so that I may me transformed into something new.

Welcome to the Crucible.

> "But he was pierced for our transgressions,
> he was crushed for our iniquities;
> the punishment that brought us peace was upon him, and
> by his wounds we are healed."
> Isaiah 53:5

The Crucible - Reflection (6 of 7)

March 21

An average melt takes 22 minutes. Be it gold or silver, I can place the necklaces, bracelets and rings into the Crucible and know that I need to check the melt after that time.

Lifting the lid of the Crucible, I'll take a carbon rod and stir the contents until I can see one thing: my reflection. It's not always easy to find. Many times, I'll stir among the "slag," squint through the smoke or jiggle the Crucible to get at it, but inevitably, there it will be; the shining metal reflecting back the image of its Refiner.

Before becoming a refiner, I read in a book somewhere, (probably Max Lucado's "On the Anvil"), that is what happens to melted metal. But until I saw it with my own eye's, I could not comprehend this beautiful outcome of the Crucible process. (I wish you could see it as well).

Just seeing myself in the liquid metal showed that the melt was ready to be poured into a new mold. But the joy I find as a refiner looking into the metal, is not in my reflection, but in the metal's radiance. Words only taint the reality of its dazzle. The melt is pure (mostly); brilliant; waiting and wanting to be used in it's new form, whatever that would be.

The Crucible has provided it's protection, it's form, it's focused heat. The Crucible has liquefied my defiance and burned off impurities. Things that would hold me back are now encased in the disposable slag. The Crucible has changed me into something new; something beautiful in God's eye's. And now, see God's reflection in me, I am ready to be used by my Savior Refiner.

Welcome to the Crucible.

The Crucible - Timing (7 of 7)

March 29

As a refiner, I can make a hefty mess of the newly molten-ed metal. Now liquid, the soup is poured out from the Crucible and into a preselected mold to cool. The timing of this move is critical. If I empty this 'new creation' too soon, the slag and metal could be malformed and be of sub-quality for use. If I allow the mass to stay in the Crucible too long, it will get stuck; never wanting to leave the comfort of it's coffin-shaped bed.

When my Savior Refiner dropped me in the Crucible on June 3rd, all I could do was trust that this inferno was merely a flicker to Him. When my Savior Refiner allowed me to experience the heat of grief and the singe of loss, all I could do was watch my pride and self-reliance melt away. And now that my Savior Refiner has poured me into a new mold, all I can do is rely on His plan and purpose. He will either keep me in the mold to 'cool' or pop me out to be used. Either way, it will be in His perfect timing.

Welcome to the Crucible.

"For I know the thoughts that I think toward you, says the Lord, thoughts of peace and not of evil, to give you a future and a hope."
Jeremiah 29:11

Good Friend's Birthday Memories

March 30

(This note is from Makenzie's friend, Katie Davis)

   A year ago today Makenzie slept over at my house for the first time.

   *A year ago today she was swimming in my pool
A year ago today she was keeping me awake all night watching pride and prejudice.*

   A year ago today she gave me my hermit crab (whom is still alive today).

   A year ago today she was playing wii with me and making me watch the raving rabbit make it's funny noises.

   A year ago today Makenzie volunteered to be the only one to sleep on the floor.

   A year ago today she ran around my pool saying "French braiding time

A year ago today she farted on my bed and she turned around and looked at us and said "sorry guys".

A year ago today she slipped in my shower and got water in her eyes.

A year ago today she ate at Don Picos with me. A year ago today she ate more cookie cake then anyone else.

A year ago today she told my mom that she was her "favorite-ist mom besides my own"

A year ago today she broke her owl necklace.

A year ago today she borrowed my shirt that says "shut up and ride". (I haven't worn it since)

A year ago today she pretended a bra was her eyes.

A year ago today she wore my bathing suit.

A year ago today she was laughing with me and setting her facebook status to "come percy we must be squeaky clean for the new world"

A year ago tomorrow she wished me happy birthday for the last time.

"HAPPY BIRTHDAY KATIE DAVIS!!! Happy birthday to you - happy birthday to you - happy birthday dear katie davis who is the most awesomest person ever.....errrrr.... - happy birthday to you!"

Wish you were here, Mak. You created the most memories out of anyone at my birthday party last year.

Makenzie and Jack

April 2

There are many things I don't remember about the days following the accident on June 3rd, '09 that claimed my daughter's life. I don't remember who came to our home to offer their unspoken condolences. I don't remember who sent which bouquet or even how our family managed to get to the church for Makenzie's Celebration Service.

I guess I have a lifetime to discover what I have already forgotten.

But one of those memory lapses came to life this evening after watching the movie "Hachiko: A Dog's Tale." It is a true story about a dog whose habit it was to wait for his master to return home from the day's events. Year after year, the dog would find his way to the same spot outside of Shibuya Train Station in Tokyo and greet his master with a wagging tale and "doggie kisses." One day, Hachiko's master did not step off the train as expected. Death had claimed his master before the day had run its course. Yet, for over ten more years, the faithful dog would sit at the station in the same spot, waiting faithfully for his master to return.

The movie touched me but not in the deep places from which tears flow. That is, until Kellie brought the movie into real life. She reminded me that the evenings following Makenzie's death, my dog, Jack would find his way to the top of our darkened stairs and lie down outside Makenzie's empty bedroom; waiting for her to come home. Eve after next, he attended the same spot; head rested on paws; snout pointed down the steps; hoping to catch a whiff of Makenzie's post-dance aroma. I would find him there; waiting; watching. Sadly, I would eventually need to speak those words to him, "Jack. She's not coming home. Come now. Let's go to bed."

Without a sound, my loyal dog would take a few steps down the staircase ... pause ... glance over his shoulder at

Makenzie's closed bedroom door and then continue his decent until he found his way to the laundry room in which he spent the night.

Tears stream uncontrollably as I write. Maybe it's because of the vividness with which this scene plays in my mind. Maybe it's because I remember that Makenzie isn't coming home. Or maybe it's because I realize that Makenzie had a profound impact on every person ... every living thing ... that knew her. Whatever. I just know that even though this weekend marks 10 months past, I will also wait with longing to see my dear Makenzie again. (Maybe Jack will be there as well).

Easter Picture

April 3

This picture is from Easter Saturday. Decorating Eggs.

We never could have guessed that this would be the last picture the five of us would take together.

I share this, not for pity, but for an invitation into the Hope that this Easter weekend gives. It is because of what Jesus did that we know we will take another family picture. But when that time comes, it won't be decorating colored eggs, it will be walking streets of gold.

Every Day is Easter in Heaven!

April 4

We have been comforted by many people over these last months after Makenzie's death. This week has provided countless opportunities for people to send their well wishes as we walked through Holy Week without Makenzie. (Another of the "firsts" that we, who have lost loved ones, must endure).

One sentiment has repeated itself from several people. "Just think. This is Makenzie's first Easter in Heaven." Truthfully, that was my thought as well because my human experience is the template through which I process life in heaven. I have no choice but to think that my daughter, Makenzie lives there but follows the time table of here.

I know better. It is not her first Easter in Heaven. She has not been counting the minutes to have an Easter Egg hunt or eat egg-bake before the sunrise service. She has not been fiddling with her Easter dress in the pew, waiting for the

Heavenly choir master to raise his arms and cue the first chord of the hymn "Jesus Christ is Risen Today!"

The truth is EVERY DAY IS EASTER IN HEAVEN! All the joy and laughter is a 24-7 deal. The pomp and circumstance is multiplied a million-fold as Makenzie, along with so many others, celebrate what Jesus has done for the entire world! The partying does not end! The dancing does not slow! The music does not wane! Makenzie is whooping it up, praising her Savior and never wanting to stop!

I can't tell you how happy and hopeful that makes me this Easter. Yes, it is another "first-without-her." Yes, I wish I could see her crack open a hard-boiled Easter egg and fish out the yoke. Yes, I would love to give her an Easter hug and hear her whisper "Happy Easter, Daddy." But how can I not be deeply, profoundly grateful to my risen Savior for letting Makenzie in on the party? How can I not worship Jesus for giving His life so that she can have hers?

If He hadn't done what He did, I would never see Makenzie again. But this Easter I celebrate because Makenzie is in my future and not in my past. And I celebrate because ...

> *"Makenzie is praising her Savior and never wanting to stop!"*

EVERY DAY IS EASTER IN HEAVEN!

The Sound of Her Voice

April 14

There is a song that plays on the radio whose opening line states, "I miss the sound of her voice." That line rehearses itself over and over in my mind as of late; "I miss the sound of her voice."

Makenzie had a beautiful voice. Not only as she sang, but simply as she spoke. Her voice revealed everything about her. Goofy phrases such as, "That was intense – just like camping," and the warm "Hi Daddy" welcomes she gave me in the hallway of our school told of a young women who loved Jesus, people, and life itself.

As more and more calendar pages are turned, the less and less I hear her voice. And the less and less I hear her voice, the more and more I desire it.

True, we have videos and recordings of her and yes, they capture the words she spoke, but they are static; frozen;

saying the same things over and over and not engaging in the day to day conversations I had with her that built our relationship. Now I speak and she doesn't answer. My words bounce off into nowhere and there is no reply. Oh, to hear one word from her but I know I'll have to wait.

"I miss the sound of her voice."

Live, Laugh, Love

April 26

I realize that there are many who stumble upon (or over) these writings as a result of a chance meeting with someone who knows Makenzie. If you are one of whom I speak, then this is for you; a quick synopsis of my little girl who is dancing with Jesus on the streets of gold.

How would you sum up your life? Photo's speak your memory. Writings tell your story. Relationships carry your legacy. Yet if you were asked what phrase would describe your existence on this earth, what would it be?

Makenzie's phrase would be "Live, Laugh, Love." I saw it in a store (again) not too long ago; carved in a rustic piece of flat board and stenciled with vines. Nice phrase, but to me ... now ... it rebirths memories of who my little girl whom God has used to change so many of us.

LIVE: Makenzie embraced life with all of its adventure and wonder; easily calling a dead bug or a dissected mink "amazing!"

LAUGH: Ok, maybe it was more of a cute snort, but Makenzie found laughter to be more of a celebration of the good rather than a reaction to the funny.

LOVE: Makenzie disliked some, but loved all. Friends and family who were easy to love, often watched from the sidelines as she found time for and loved on those to whom society had placed off the center. People who were new at school or who had isolated themselves for whatever reason couldn't escape her bouncing into their world with a friendly, "Hey guys!"

All of this ... Live, Laugh, Love ... grew out of the core relationship in her life. That core was not me; not her mom, brother or sister. Not friends or other family. Makenzie's core relationship was (and is) with this guy.

His name is Jesus. And He makes life worth living (oh, and loving).

What would your life phrase be?

Happy Birthday

May 3

Today is Makenzie's birthday. (If I'd forgotten, her friends' posts on Facebook would've reminded me – Thank you).

I think back to last year's birthday and thought that my daughter was weird. We asked her if she wanted to have a party to celebrate her 18th birthday. We asked her if she wanted to "do it up grand" but instead, all she wanted was to be with Kellie, Nathan, Maddie, Grandpa, Grandma and me. Didn't matter what we did. Didn't matter where we went. She simply wanted to be with the people who loved her most. Weird.

So we packed up a picnic and headed to the beach; just the seven of us; the perfect number to celebrate a perfect day. Fighting the salted-infused breeze, we lit the candles, slaughtered THE SONG, and munched on a Sam's Club, hand crafted, glazed lemon cake. Simple. Beautiful. Holy. Weird.

"By being beautifully different, she was wonderfully weird"

Today, we don't have any candles; no cake or picnic. We didn't wake up, pull out our family's Celebration Plate on which would be her birthday breakfast. We didn't sneak up to her room, jump on her bed and wake her up by yelling "Happy Birthday!" All we have this year are the well wishes of her dear friends and family, the memory of birthday's past and the pictures that support them.

But for us, that is enough. Because for 18 years, we raised the amazing girl whom God entrusted to us. A girl who loved her Maker. A girl who changed our lives. A girl who, by being beautifully different, was wonderfully weird.

Happy Birthday, my dearest princess.

Changing the Lyrics

May 6

If I let my thoughts wander, setting them adrift on the breeze of the past, often, they come to rest on Makenzie's love of music. This morning, they recall a song that sprang from her 6th grade lips every time we were driving in the car. Her favorite — my favorite —FFH's "One of These Days."

A snippet of lyrics reads:

> *One of these days*
> *Gonna see the hand that took the nails for me*
> *One of these days*
> *Gonna hold the key to the mansion built for me*
> *One of these days*
> *Gonna walk the streets of gold that were paved for me*
> *One of these days*
> *I'm gonna see my Savior face to face*
> *One of these days*

This morning, my thoughts paint the new lyrics that Makenzie now sings:

Even today
I can see the hand that took the nails for me
Even today
I can hold the key to the mansion built for me
Even today
I'm walking the streets of gold that were paved for me
Even today
I can see my Savior face to face
Even today

I can't wait to sing the changed lyrics with her. Someday ... someday.

I Want More Pictures

May 12

I've poured over them. I've studied them. I've printed, emailed, posted and cropped them. They arc the pictures I have of Makenzie. I know every shadow and line of her face in the photos and they remind me of the joy and full life that she lead.

As of late, Kellie and I are longing for NEW pictures. We scanned the full Senior Class picture from her high school but didn't find her twinkling eyes or wide teethed smile in the midst of the faces. We looked at the end of the year Facebook pictures from her friends but she was not in them.

What we'd give to see her on her last day of High School. How we long for those photos which would tell us that her life with us was continuing. But they are not there.

Don't get me wrong. We are very grateful for the pictures and video that we have;

> "We are very grateful for the pictures that we have"

especially from Caitlin and the last photo shoot. But to see her in a graduation robe, playfully grabbing the tassel with her tongue, would be an incredible gift.

I wonder if there are camera's in Heaven; to capture the events and experiences that we will have with her. Probably not. But just being with her again — with everyone again — gathered around Jesus' throne — will be the ultimate photo op!

The Last Prom Night

May 13

Kellie so beautifully described our experience with Makenzie's last prom which happened this night a year ago. Read this from a mother's heart:

A year ago today, Makenzie was attending her first and little did we know, her last prom of high school. I have special memories of preparing for that evening with her from helping to make the video asking her childhood friend Alex to fly down to prom in Houston, picking out the dress, getting the shoes, getting her hair done with Annie, flowers and what they would all do back at our house and the next day at the beach. I replay in my head the fun conversations we had and the enthusiasm she had about everything.

Makenzie helped her friend, Wes in creatively asking her dance buddy, Shelby, to go with him. Makenzie was so excited to give him ideas and even more excited that Shelby said yes! Todd and I borrowed our friends' Suburban to drive the group around and planned the evening with "Dinner on the Dock" of his parent's place, a stop off at Main Event for bowling (in their prom dresses/tuxes) and then a full-stay-up till the wee hours of the morning/ breakfast at our house for Makenzie, Alex, Wes, Shelby, Emilie & Zane.

We were the Chauffeurs for the evening and LOVED it. Each part of was met with Makenzie's giggles of glee. I can hear that distinct Makenzie giggle in my mind now. She was so excited about the entire evening and everything was always, "amazing" to her. How weird that our 18 year old didn't mind her parents toting everyone around and having as much fun planning and carrying out the event as she had.

I've thought much over the past 11 months of the gifts of time we had with Makenzie spanning her 18 years of life. We've talked as a family about the last few years at LSA where we were all there together; the kids in school and Todd and I on staff. The moments are valuable in my mind and time I will never again have on this Earth with my daughter because of the tragic evening of June 3rd, 2009.

Tonight is prom at LSA in Houston, then their Senior trip to Florida and graduation. Although I am glad for her class and I know all these things will be fun, it is one more reminder of how difficult it would have been for us to stay in Houston, seeing all of them and Makenzie not being there. I've also pondered how blessed we are in knowing that Makenzie is in heaven. Not looking down wishing she were back here, but rejoicing with the King of Kings in the ultimate dance that supersedes any prom here on Earth. What do people do without that knowledge and without Christ? You are either living for God or living for yourself and the second doesn't get you anywhere.

Tonight I thank God for my Makenzie. For the special moments we had as a Mom and daughter. I pray for her friends that do not know Christ as Savior and the lives they are leading separate from Him. One day, they will have to

> *"What do people do who don't know Christ?"*

choose. Tonight I will be praying for safety for Makenzie's friends at LSA and for the faculty as well! There will be one less dancer on the dance floor. But for Makenzie, her dance is being completed in heaven.

Just A Simple Kiss

May 19

There is something special about a gentle kiss that Daddy receives from Daughter. Those innocent lips smacking against a well-seasoned, gruffy cheek, communicates sweetness ... connection ... love. Just A Simple Kiss.

I loved that kiss from her. Usually it comes unexpectedly. Hurrying off to school. Driving into the drop off lane. Suddenly, she grabs my shoulder sleeve, pulls me sideways and plants one. I can't help but smile and say, "I love you, sweets." "Love you too, Daddy." Then, she bee-bops out of the car, joining her friends and disappearing behind the glass doors that would keep her safe for the balance of her day.

And I just sit there; thinking, How can I be so blessed with a beautiful daughter who surprises me with her simple kiss. Then, as if being jolted out of a dream, the driver behind, gently taps on her horn. As I drive away, I am reminded about past moments like these with Makenzie.   But today's hurrying, drop-off, grab and kiss came from my other daughter, Maddie, who told me she loved me, with just A Simple Kiss.

The Ultimate Graduation

May 22

High School Graduation. A defining moment on the time line that is our lives.

Last night, our Makenzie graduated from Lutheran South Academy in Houston. Wait ... Let me rephrase that. Makenzie's Name graduated from the school. The idea for this edit comes from the bulletin that was handed out at the occasion.

Turning to the back of the two-fold, the list of graduates neatly appears in two columns. Some names are simply listed. Others with an asterisk noting "Magna Cum Laude" or "Cum Laude." (These are Latin phrases which denote academic honors). There was a third title that only one person held last night. It was not designated with an alphabetic punctuation. The special honor was highlighted with a cross. "Graduated to be with our Lord."

That is how Makenzie was honored. The ultimate graduation for her ... for any of us. Kellie and I received her diploma during the

☦ *"Makenzie Stocker Graduated to be with our Lord"*

special presentation portion of the night. Tears of happiness and loss dripped down our cheeks as we opened the placard to see her name. My first thought was Kenzie's gonna love seeing this!

It is difficult to even write about this. My eyes moisten as I remember last night and my futile attempt to find Makenzie's face in the sea of green robes and tassels. But I am reminded that she is with Jesus. She has graduated based on the work of her Savior not on the work of her studies. My lovely graduate is home.

Handling the Anniversary

June 3

The back-corner table of my local coffee shop. I don't remember how I got here. Today, my thoughts are filled by my daughter, Makenzie, and on the whirlwind journey on which we've traveled since her death, one year ago today.

Now, I don't remember even ordering my half-calf, dark-roast coffee only seconds ago; but, no matter. I am allowing the deep numbness to press tears which moisten my eyes and I shake my head not believing that the unbelievable has happened to me.

I haven't had a day like this for a very long time.

My schedule is cleared because I know what the next hours will hold. I will think about Makenzie's last words to me only moments before entering the intersection that marks her death. (6 min before: "I love you, Daddy. I'm on my way home"). I will replay the memory of Kellie, Nathan,

Maddie and me huddling and weeping together on our bed after telling them that their sister will never be coming home. I will feel the warmth of our family and friends as I remember how they wailed with us. I will ponder how our life is so, so different and how this Crucible of loss has reshaped us. I will wander through the hundreds of comments, emails and midnight messages that her dear friends have penned on her Facebook and be amazed that my little girl had such a huge effect on so many. And I will contemplate the emptiness and hopelessness of those whose daughters, sons and friends have died without knowing Jesus personally. I don't have that emptiness. I know that Makenzie only cut in line on my journey with and toward my Savior.

Mostly, I will sense God. I will walk with Him today; more closely, more intently, more slowly. I will remember that Makenzie's death did not take Him by surprise and that He has allowed something that Satan meant for evil to be turned into good.

Ultimately ... in my sorrow and pain that marks today, in my desperate longing to hold her again and experience her joy ... I will praise my Lord, Jesus because He continues to turn my mourning into dancing.

8:08 PM

June 3

good night, my sweet button nose ...

see ya soon.

daddy.

A Painting from Heaven

June 7

Our dear friend, Diane Bean, commissioned local artist
Kevin Beilfuss to paint a picture of Makenzie. Even
though he never met her, Kevin captured her spirit, her joy
and her love of dance through simple paint applied on a
canvass. Our family is ever grateful to both Diane and
Kevin for this painting from heaven.

(You can see more of Kevin's work at
www.kevinbeilfuss.com)

Another Box

June 19

As we sort through the mountains of boxes that have defined our life, we are stumbling upon all of Makenzie's stuff that we packed up shortly after her death. Another box ... Another memory. Another bin, another bag, another drawer, another Father's Day card; they all remind me of her.

I found her baby box this morning. Small and simple, I didn't want to open it but knew that it would be good for me to do so. I lifted the lid and saw her baby footprint on a little card no bigger that a dollar, folded in half. I hooked my pinky around the small hospital band that cuffed her baby ankle only moments after she was born. I read a simple white card, stamped with the words, "From Your God-Parents".

So many boxes. So many joys. So many memories that help me remember Makenzie's short life that has such long impact. Yet, while the pain of last year has subsided, the ache gnaws on; especially when opening another box.

> " Her short life had a long impact "

Sharing Her Story

June 22

Someone made the comment, "Now that Makenzie's class has graduated and will be moving to different parts of the globe, just think about how many more will hear her story!" I hadn't thought of that. I hadn't wrapped my brain around the fact that part of her senior class's story is her life, death and life.

I can hear the conversations:

"... and there was this one girl who died before senior year."

"... Makenzie use to wiggle through me and my boyfriend and say 'Make room for Jesus'. But I never got mad; she was just cool that way."

"... before her death I didn't really get this God-stuff. Now it's all different."

As I think about her influence, I only pray that the relationships that I have — that I develop — will have a deeper meaning than sharing a cup of coffee and talking about current events. I pray that for you as well, friend. Because when all is said and done, a full life is defined not by the quantity of your possessions, but by the quality of your relationships.

American Girl

July 1

(A note from Kellie)

While unpacking things that have been packed for the last year, I stumbled upon all of Makenzie's American Girl things. She had Kirsten and all the trinkets & clothes that went with Kirsten. Her Grandma bought her most everything...the horse, the violin (mini), bed, clothing, background scenes and settings. You get the idea. Amidst all this stuff I found a book Makenzie had. It's called "The Taking Care and Keeping of Me". It was a journal/book she received when she was 12 years old. On the pages titled, "Who Am I?" this is what she wrote to the statements that were listed. Ironically, she wrote this on June 3, 2003, six years before the day she would go to heaven.

Inside and out, here's what makes me uniquely me:

" First of all I have Jesus. I know where I am going when I die. Second, I am in great shape, *not overweight, not a lot of zits or anything like that. God made me a beautiful girl. I love my family, I have real true friends. I face my problems. And I have lots of talent. I love music. I am a ballet-dance-a-holic. I love what I do! I want to become a professional dancer when I grow up. But what's unique about ME... I am forgiven and I love my Father Jesus."*

I loved reading this. In most everything Makenzie wrote about she talked about Jesus and who she was in Christ. What I saw in this writing at her tender young age when everything was changing, was a realness of who Makenzie was and what she knew about herself. It makes me smile.

There are still tears as I go through her things, but the joy is there too. Joy came to me tonight after reading this. Then I received a text from Kim Hatch in Houston (mom of sweet

Jackson & beautiful Olivia who was one of the recipients of Makenzie's named scholarships). She texted, "Jackson is packed for camp with Makenzie's picture in his trunk and her story in his heart. He plans on sharing her story with everyone and since he knows no stranger, I am sure he will. Her ripples keep going and going..." Thanks, Kim for sharing your joy in your precious son.

Maybe you have sadness or loss in your life. Or just struggles that are messy. It sounds so simple and yet it is life changing...turn to Jesus. Not a religion but a relationship with Him.

There's Healing in the Speaking

July 15

For me, there is healing in speaking. Each time I share Makenzie's life with others, a small edge of pain is chipped away. Like a sculptor's chisel on the surface of marble, each "Makenzie" word I speak helps notch a groove in the stone of my ache.

And what has been amazing to me is that I see the Master Artist at work through the telling and re-telling of an amazing young woman whose life and death affected so many. Stories still stream in. Messages still ping her Facebook. Emails still make account of how Makenzie has inspired people to re-prioritize their lives. All bear witness to God's ability to turn pain into purpose.

"God can turn pain into purpose"

So I'll tell her story again. It stinks that I have a story like this to tell. But as He gives me opportunity, I will accept the speaking engagements to talk about a life cut short in order for others to live long.

"I tell you the truth, unless a kernel of wheat falls to the ground and dies, it remains only a single seed. But if it dies, it produces many seeds."
John 12:24

Texas to Louisiana to Kenya, Africa

July 25

How is it that one, sweet 18 year old from Houston can reach thousands with her simple life of loving Jesus? If she knew how many people God is changing through her life-death-life story, she'd be amazed.

A week ago, Kellie shared Makenzie's story with over 25,000 high school students at the National Youth Gathering. These young adults are changed forever. From the event, they are texting their parents telling them, "I love you Daddy." They are re-prioritizing their lives to make it about God and not them. They are realizing that God loves them even in the midst of life's storms.

Right now, there are several dozen African kids in Kenya, learning what it means to dance for an audience of One. Through the ministry of Starfish Kenya, young people are donning white "Makenzie" dresses and twirling away before the Lord in worship.

Awesome ... Holy ...

These stories and the many Facebooks, emails, and text messages that we received help relieve the ache when Makenzie went home. Our mourning is being changed to joy; one story ... one conversation ... one life at a time.

Please keep the Starfish Kenya team in prayer!

Wish You Were Here

August 18

Post cards sport the phrase, "Miss You - Wish You Were Here." The "Miss You" looks to yesterday — the "Wish You Were Here" looks to today. The former is in the past... the latter is in the present. And so it goes with my ache.

I don't miss Makenzie so much anymore. Shocking for you to read. Healthy for me to write. Obviously, I could intentionally wallow in empty spot at our table or the loss of all that joy, but today I am relegated to wishing she were here.

I wish Makenzie was here to see how beautiful and fun her younger sister has become. I wish Makenzie was around to hear her brother's "voice" in and through his music. I wish she was here to see how close her mom and dad have become; to witness the leaves change, to take long walks with me, to meet the incredible people that have followed her story and to experience the countless other events that have made our lives beautiful.

All in all, I wish others could meet her and experience a young woman who knew her centering was in Jesus.

Wish You Were Here, button-nose.

A New Direction

October 22

A chunk of days has passed since I've sat down to post a blog. Turns out, my new normal has demanded not only my time, but also my focus ... and that's a good thing. Because it is God's provision to help my life move forward.

The tangible memories of my loss do not sneak up on me anymore. Makenzie's bobby-pins have made their way out of the nooks and crannies of my car. The stamp of her fingers that donned my inside windshield has all but faded. And her belongings have found their asylum in a corner of our basement.

All of this shows me that God's Holy Spirit has brought me through an intense crucible experience, has poured me into a mold and is now re-forming my life to be used for His purpose. I don't know what that completely looks like but for now, it is enough to know that He is in control.

I will keep this blog alive more as a devotional but not necessarily Makenzie focused. The change in the blog reflects the change in me. My Lord has taken me through the worst of the darkness. He has shown me that a life solely dependent on Him is a life well lived. He has rescued me from the pit of grief and set me on a new journey. And my loving Lord is showing me how to turn pain in to purpose.

Thank you, my friends, for journeying with me. Thank you for your comments of strength. Thank you for your insights and stories. It has been my pleasure to share with you what I pray you never have to experience. But if (or maybe I should say 'when') you find yourself dining at the table of tragedy, remember that God is in the chair right next to you. He knows how the meal is served and he'll always bus your table of fear and pain.